## Praise for *Releasing What Isn't Yours*

"Wise and visionary. Laurel is a pioneer in healing and includes the essential dimension of the sacred that has been missing for so many."

**Jack Kornfield**
author of *A Path with Heart* and *All in This Together*

"*Releasing What Isn't Yours* invites us to explore the many layers of experience that often go unrecognized in everyday life—and in psychotherapy—yet influence us in profound ways. Laurel Parnell is our deeply insightful, wise, and courageous guide whose devotion to healing and illuminating the truth are revealed in this inspirational personal and professional journey to uncover the ways we are inextricably connected across time and space. When these energy patterns go unrecognized, we may become stuck in the chaos and rigidity of the impaired integration of unresolved trauma. Introducing us to the origins and practical steps of her approach of Multidimensional Integrative Healing, the chapters of this book provide useful ways of understanding layers of experience—whether they are mechanisms or metaphors of the mind—that we can tap into to cultivate post-traumatic growth and resilience in our liberated lives."

**Daniel J. Siegel, MD**
*New York Times* bestselling author of *Aware* and *Mind*

"This book serves as both a map and an invitation: a map for understanding how healing can unfold across physical, emotional, somatic, psychological, and spiritual realms; and an invitation to trust the innate intelligence within each of us that moves toward wholeness when given the right support.

Laurel's writing is grounded, wise, and accessible, making complex multidimensional concepts feel natural and empowering.

For anyone who has experienced trauma, for clinicians seeking to expand their therapeutic repertoire, or for spiritual practitioners longing for a bridge between profound inner experience and psychological integration, this book is a gift. Laurel Parnell has once again illuminated a path toward reclaiming our authenticity, our agency, and the radiant presence of our True Self."

**Diane Poole Heller, PhD**

author of *The Power of Attachment* and *Healing Your Attachment Wounds*, creator of the Dynamic Attachment Re-patterning experience (DARe) approach, founder of Trauma Solutions

"In this revolutionary guidebook, Laurel Parnell offers an artful synthesis that unites ancient wisdom with contemporary trauma healing. *Releasing What Isn't Yours* integrates decades of her pioneering EMDR teaching and illuminates ways to heal trauma as a doorway to our True Nature—that unchanging essence which is already whole and free within us. This is a cutting-edge book that helps us discover where awakening and therapeutic healing converge—an important contribution. Highly recommended for anyone looking for support to live an authentic life."

**Loch Kelly, MDiv, LCSW**

author of *Shift into Freedom* and creator of the Mindful Glimpses app

"Laurel Parnell has written the most accessible and practical book addressing EMDR, spirituality, energetic boundaries, dreamwork, and more.

She has provided a new integrative roadmap to help all of us address multidimensional problems. As a leading therapist and trainer, Laurel has once again shed light on such underrepresented topics as shamanism in combination with therapy and how to release unwanted spirit attachments. Most importantly, Laurel has given us all the tools to align with our TRUE SELF when facing any distress. This is a highly compelling book and a must-have for therapists and clients alike."

**Jennifer Freed, PhD**
bestselling author of *A Map to Your Soul*

"The great alchemical formula of spiritual practice is turning our suffering into compassion and wisdom. *Releasing What Isn't Yours* is a powerful example of how one can transform tragedy into a gift that will benefit many. Laurel Parnell went through one of the most painful human experiences imaginable. Through her journey of healing, this skillful and highly respected therapist integrated a number of supportive modalities into an original and profound therapeutic approach. I highly recommend this book."

**James Baraz**
co-author of *Awakening Joy*, co-founder of Spirit Rock Meditation Center in Woodacre, California

"A pioneer in the fields of EMDR and transpersonal psychology, Dr. Parnell's life was turned upside down with the traumatic loss of her adult son to violence. This catalyzed an unconventional and profound healing journey that led her to engage with some of the deepest dimensions of the human psyche. This book is the fruit of that journey—an original, multidimensional, and integrative approach that offers a wide range of subtle healing modalities for the general public as well as therapists. Dr. Parnell's dedication, sensitivity, and love radiate in every page, empowering readers' self-healing and trust in their inner knowing."

**John J. Prendergast, PhD**
author of *Your Deepest Ground*, *The Deep Heart*, and *In Touch*

# Releasing What Isn't Yours

## Also by Laurel Parnell

**Books**

*Rewiring the Addicted Brain with EMDR-Based Treatment*

*Attachment-Focused EMDR: Healing Relational Trauma*

*Tapping In: A Step-by-Step Guide to Activating Your Healing Resources Through Bilateral Stimulation*

*A Therapist's Guide to EMDR*

*EMDR in the Treatment of Adults Abused as Children*

*Transforming Trauma: EMDR*

**Audio**

*Tapping In: A Step-by-Step Guide to Activating Your Healing Resources Through Bilateral Stimulation*

# Releasing What Isn't Yours

## Living from Your True Self Through Multidimensional Integrative Healing

Laurel Parnell, PhD

ST. MARTIN'S ESSENTIALS
NEW YORK

First published in the United States by St. Martin's Essentials,
an imprint of St. Martin's Publishing Group

*EU Representative:* Macmillan Publishers Ireland Ltd, 1st Floor, The Liffey Trust Centre, 117–126 Sheriff Street Upper, Dublin 1, D01 YC43



This book is not intended as a substitute for the medical recommendations of physicians, mental health professionals, or other health-care providers. Rather, it is intended to offer information to help the reader cooperate with physicians, mental health professionals, and health-care providers in a mutual quest for optimal well-being. We advise readers to carefully review and understand the ideas presented and to seek the advice of a qualified professional before attempting to use them.

Book design by Rachael Murray

www.stmartins.com

The Library of Congress Cataloging-in-Publication Data is available upon request.

ISBN 978-1-64963-442-9 (trade paperback)
ISBN 978-1-64963-443-6 (ebook)



First Edition: 2026

10 9 8 7 6 5 4 3 2 1

This book is dedicated to the loving memory
of my son Catono Raymond Perez

May this book bring greater love and healing to the vast, multidimensional web that we are all a part of, radiating out in all directions, including to the past and future generations.

# Contents

Introduction to Multidimensional Integrative Healing 1

**Part One** Setting the Foundation: Background and Development of Multidimensional Integrative Healing

1 Spiritual Influences and Teachers 17

2 EMDR and Its Evolution 25

3 Multicultural Experience 35

4 My Son's Death and My Healing Journey 43

**Part Two** Accessing the Resources of Multidimensional Integrative Healing

5 Your Four Foundational Resources 53

6 Spiritual and Natural Resources 71

7 Ancestral Resources 91

**Part Three** Developing Energetic Sovereignty

8 Basic Tools for Energetic Sovereignty 111

9 Working with Energetic Cords 129

10 Working with the True Self 145

11 Bringing Together Multidimensional Integrative Healing Practices 157

**Part Four** Dimensions of Spirit Work

12 The Importance of Dreamwork in Multidimensional Integrative Healing 169

13 EMDR and After-Death Communication 179

14 Recognizing and Assessing Spirit Attachments 189

15 Acknowledgment and Ritual to Facilitate Spirit Release 201

Concluding Thoughts 219

Acknowledgments 223

Multidimensional Integrative Healing Practices 227

Notes 231

About the Author 233

# Introduction to Multidimensional Integrative Healing

Multidimensional Integrative Healing (MDIH) was born out of the tragic death of my son, which broke me apart, sending me on a journey of healing that called for everything I knew to do as an expert in trauma recovery, as well as all that I had learned through a lifetime of spiritual practice and insights. Even with all that I knew to do and the support I had, I found I needed to expand beyond to spiritual sources to experience the healing I needed. This healing came from a wise, compassionate, and highly skilled spirit worker who not only helped mend the brokenness but also taught me ways of healing that I have been able to bring to others. I view this MDIH work as a tapestry of many strands that weave together my understanding about life, psychology, diverse cultures, healing, somatic and energy work, spirituality, Eye Movement Desensitization and Reprocessing (EMDR), and transpersonal psychotherapy. This book presents many of these different strands and practical ways you can recognize and use for your own healing multidimensionally.

## What Is Multidimensional Integrative Healing?

Multidimensional Integrative Healing (MDIH) is a powerful approach to healing and personal empowerment that supports our innate healing intelligence and its capacity to move us toward health and wholeness. Acknowledging, accessing, and supporting the innate healing intelligence and drive toward wholeness are fundamental to MDIH. The theoretical framework of the method integrates information and practices from transpersonal psychology, Eye Movement Desensitization and Reprocessing (EMDR), Attachment-Focused EMDR (AF-EMDR), Eastern spiritual practices, shamanic and spirit work, energy work, and mystical traditions of the world. Because of this, I'll be referencing this range of knowledge, methods, and practices throughout the book as I share an understanding of the MDIH method and how you can personally engage with it as part of your (or your client's) personal practice. Most of the information and practices presented in this book derive from teachings I received from my spiritual teachers and mentors as well as personal experience, not information from books. Because most of what I have learned is from my teachers who imparted their wisdom to me orally, and their teachings and spiritual practices have multiple sources and lineages, I cannot direct you to references for the source of their teachings. There are certainly things you might read from some of my teachers (Lama Thubten Yeshe, Jean Klein, Suzanne Segal, Jack Kornfield, Jean Schneider), but I did not learn what you will find in these pages from books.

## Contributors to Multidimensional Integrative Healing

Important contributors to MDIH include:

- **Transpersonal psychology** integrates traditional psychological approaches with experiences that expand beyond the personal level and include spiritual and transcendent experiences. This branch of psychology includes the ethical principles that govern the practice of psychotherapy for psychologists and other mental health professionals.

- **Eye Movement Desensitization and Reprocessing (EMDR)**, developed by the psychologist Francine Shapiro, is used for healing traumas with the use of alternating bilateral stimulation on activated memory networks.

- **Attachment-Focused EMDR (AF-EMDR)**, developed by this author, evolved from standard EMDR. It includes the use of resources to support trauma healing but also for repair of developmental and ancestral traumas.

- **Mahayana Buddhism** is a major branch of Buddhism developed in ancient India that focuses on the importance of compassion and service. Mahayana Buddhism emphasizes the bodhisattva ideal where one's goal is to become enlightened for the sake of all beings. In this branch of Buddhism, the belief is that everyone has the potential to awaken to their True Nature.

- **Tibetan Buddhism**, also known as Vajrayana Buddhism, is another major branch of Buddhism that originated in Tibet. Tibetan Buddhism includes elements of Mahayana Buddhism emphasizing compassion, service, and the bodhisattva ideal, as well as tantric practices that make use of visualization of deities and mantras. The role of the guru or teacher is also important, providing guidance, blessings, and inspiration. Tibetan Buddhism was mostly practiced in Tibet and Bhutan until the Chinese invasion in 1959, when thousands of Tibetans fled, bringing their practices to countries around the world.

- **Vipassana, or mindfulness meditation**, is a simple technique that has been practiced in Asia for more than 2,600 years. The practice begins with the focusing of attention on the breath; then thoughts, feelings, body sensations, and sounds are dispassionately noticed without judgment. The practice allows us to see through the mind's conditioning and thereby to be more fully present in the moment. We disidentify with the objects of awareness, which arise and pass away out of silence, as these objects that we have heretofore imagined creating a self now are seen to have no substance. This insight creates freedom from self-identification and great peace.

- **Shamanic and spirit work practices** and beliefs from various regions in the world emphasize empowering the individual rather than the practitioner. One of the oldest forms of spirituality and healing that predates organized religions, shamanistic practices and beliefs are found in cultures worldwide, including in parts of Asia, Tibet, Oceania, and North and South America. Shamanic practices use drumming, rattling, and chanting to induce altered states of consciousness to commune with the spirit world and facilitate healing.

- **Energy work** includes techniques for assessing energy, creating boundaries, grounding, releasing energetic attachments, and increasing energetic sovereignty.

- **Nondual spirituality** is the understanding or direct experience that there is a pure, unifying consciousness that is boundaryless and infinite and out of which all phenomena arise and pass away. There is no separation between self and other, as all are manifestations of the same consciousness. It is this Pure Consciousness that illumines all life. All things are seen as interconnected and part of a greater whole. Advaita Vedanta, a school of Hindu philosophy, and Tibetan Buddhism include nondual teaching.

- **A cross-cultural perspective that is open and accepting of many ways of viewing life** expands our understanding of how people from different cultures think, feel, act, and believe. It helps us acknowledge that culture influences human behavior and ways in which we view the world. It helps us appreciate different perspectives and viewpoints and increases our awareness of how our own cultural background can bias our perceptions and interpretations of people from cultures that differ from our own.

- **Nature-based spirituality** emphasizes the sacredness of nature and the interconnectedness of all living things. Practices include ways to connect to nature that provide resources for strength, grounding, and healing.

## The Influence of Different Dimensions for Healing

Multidimensional Integrative Healing recognizes that multiple dimensions of reality and experience exist and can be accessed for healing. These dimensions include:

- **the physical world**, such as the earth, trees, water, and air on our planet

- **the psychological and emotional dimension** includes information we carry in our nervous systems from experiences throughout our lives

- **the somatic dimension**—the experiences that are stored in our bodies

- **the spiritual dimension**, such as spiritual experiences of something larger than us, wisdom, compassion for self and others, psychic experiences, and helping spirits (including angelic beings, power animals, and familial ancestors)

This approach understands that realms that exist beyond this world and life continues beyond the physical body. Ancestral information, including traumas and beliefs, can affect an individual's emotional and psychological state in the present, whether we are aware of the source of the information or not.

## Addressing Blockages to Your True Self

Multidimensional Integrative Healing supports the individual's wisdom, inner knowing, and felt sense of truth. As therapists and healers, we work to strengthen and align with our clients' inner knowing. We don't impose or do things for the client; rather, we help them find their own resources that can be called upon for help when needed. The work empowers clients and supports their personal and energetic sovereignty. As therapists, we align with our clients' inner knowing. We don't impose on them our concepts or interpretations. We ask them what they need instead of telling them what we think they need.

In this book you will learn many methods for healing. These practices can be used by therapists or healers with clients or for direct use by those of you who find them helpful for yourself. The orientation in MDIH is on supporting your inner knowing and energetic sovereignty. Here you'll explore and discover what works for you. You are the expert on yourself. The questions asked of you here will help you to unlock your knowing.

I have found in over thirty years of clinical practice using Eye Movement Desensitization and Reprocessing (EMDR) that not only is it a powerful and effective therapy for healing trauma but it also opens people to transpersonal experiences. In our efforts toward healing, I will share a lot about EMDR as a part of MDIH. EMDR is a therapy that clears emotional charge and that which isn't True Self. EMDR releases old conditioning that holds dysfunctional patterns in the mind and body. When we use EMDR on these places that are old and emotionally charged, they move out; they are freed, and what is true and healthy is strengthened. Our True Self is like the sun that is always shining but is obscured by clouds. When we focus awareness on the clouds and add bilateral stimulation—a therapeutic technique involving alternating stimulation from the right side and left side of the body, which is a part of the practice of EMDR—those clouds begin to dissipate, burning off like fog that lifts with the morning sunshine. What is revealed when the clouds disperse is the True Self, which manifests as love, compassion, wisdom, joy, creative expression, and a sense of wholeness.

These clouds, or blocks to True Self, can be conditioning created from experiences in a person's history and development. They can also have other causes that require additional tools to supplement what we do in our EMDR work. In my experience, these additional blockages can be associated with things such as these:

- past-life experiences that impact functioning in the present
- energies that do not belong to the individual that have attached to them
- energetic attachments to others that bind and create problems in a person's life
- ancestral or intergenerational traumas
- soul or spirit loss that occurs after a near-death experience or severe trauma

EMDR can be thought of as a method to integrate information that is not integrating on its own. I have used bilateral stimulation to link the past with the present, the child self with the adult self, and the consequences of problematic behaviors with the behavior. I have also found that it can be used to integrate spiritual experiences, including from near-death experiences, and to reintegrate soul or spirit parts that have left because of trauma. I also suspect that bilateral stimulation acts to clear the veil to other dimensions of reality. Drumming, dancing, and rattling (all forms of bilateral stimulation) have all been used to induce altered states in many traditions. In chapter 10 you will see examples of how EMDR was used to help access the True Self at the conclusion of an EMDR session and in chapter 13 how it was used to elicit after-death communications.

## A History of My Work and Multidimensional Integrative Healing

While I am eager to share my work and gathered knowledge here, it has at times felt risky for me as a licensed clinical psychologist. With so much emphasis placed on what is called evidence-based practice, anything that does not have research to support it seems to lose credibility. Yet so much of what we do in healing work is not measurable. When we begin to innovate or expand into areas that are in the realm of the transpersonal, we may lose our standing as legitimate healers. As far back as 1997, when my first book, *Transforming Trauma: EMDR*, was about to be published, Francine Shapiro contacted me and urged me to stop the publication. Because I had written about the transpersonal/spiritual experiences my clients had reported, she feared EMDR (which already was seen as questionable because of the use of eye movements) would lose all credibility. She told me that my book would "destroy EMDR." My publisher thankfully did not share her concern and published it around the same time as Shapiro's *EMDR: The Breakthrough "Eye Movement" Therapy for Overcoming Anxiety, Stress, and Trauma* was released.

Multidimensional Integrative Healing, however, expands even further from my earlier writing. I realize, too, that much of the fear for those of us writing about non-ordinary reality and spiritual experiences derives from the constraints of the culture we abide in and our profession is in turn influenced by. The more I have explored, worked with, and witnessed my clients' experiences, the more I have opened to and learned about multidimensional reality and the vast mystery of human expression, including how constrained I am by colonialist thinking and worldview.

Colonization occurred thousands of years ago in Europe when Christianity arrived, and those that practiced nature-based spirituality were either killed or converted. This same colonization was brought to the Americas, Africa, and other places around the world where the invaders seized not only land but also the minds of the people. This colonization of the mind—according to the Kenyan novelist Ngugi wa Thiong'o—is a comprehensive process designed to make its victims "ashamed of their names, history, systems of belief, languages, lore, art, dance, song, sculpture, even the color of their skin."[1] This happened to people of color but also to the original people of Europe who lost their spirituality to survive, who then later became invaders themselves, colonizing others by imposing their worldview wherever they went.

Since 1995 I have taught EMDR nationally and internationally. I have spent time with people from many cultures around the world and have been exposed to other ways of viewing life. When we leave places that are heavily influenced by colonial views, we see that the people and cultures are very familiar with multidimensional reality; it is how they already live. For example, when I teach in Singapore—with people from India, China, and Malaysia who are not Christianized—and I talk about past lives, energetic attachments, soul or spirit loss, or ancestral resources or entanglements, I am speaking about things that are part of their lived experience. Hindu East Indians are very familiar with calling on deities to help with problems and to provide support when needed. When doing EMDR, some of these clients connect with the deities that are part of their family's spiritual practice. Perhaps the family has an altar to Kali, the Hindu goddess that embodies the power of creation and destruction in one entity. Ancestral worship and recognition of spirits or souls that may not have crossed over are also part of their worldview.

However, in the Americas, this is not the case, especially for Indigenous people who have been imprisoned in residential schools, stripped of their names, hair, language, spirituality, and families. Shamed, abused, and Christianized, they were brainwashed into accepting the perpetrator's religion, as they had no other choice.

This indoctrination continues to this day, and the people struggle to find their way back to the traditions that supported them for thousands of years. This struggle became apparent to me when talking with an Indigenous elder who is an EMDR-trained licensed mental health professional about her experiences with her clients. As she spoke about some of the methods she has used with her clients, such as helping to release a soul of a deceased person who had attached to her client, she told me she was afraid that if she were found out, she could lose her license. She felt constrained by what was allowed in the dominant culture. She told me she was a product of the residential school system and carried the traumas of that experience. She felt bound by the colonialist views and doctrines that still threatened her ability to practice using all that she knew to do, including methods that had been passed down for generations.

I want to invite you, the readers of this book, to decolonize your mind. Recognize that the worldview you carry is limited to the culture within which you reside. There is a much wider world of experience that people carry and are afraid to speak about in the United States and much of the Western world for fear of being pathologized, misdiagnosed as psychotic or crazy, shunned, shamed, or deemed unprofessional or fringe. Clients will not tell their therapists things they experience because of their fear of judgment. I want to emphasize here that our work as healers is not to interpret a person's experience but to open our mind to the variety of human experience and to recognize that there are multiple dimensions of reality beyond what we know or can know. This opening to the mystery is key, I think. When I am open, my clients can report to me their experience, I can help them with the tools I have, and I can aid them in coming to their own understanding or formulation.

We are living in times when many people are opening their minds to new ways of viewing life. There is more mixing of cultures and exchange of perspectives. The questioning of structures, such as the effects of colonization worldwide, is opening us to the effects on our thinking and views of reality.

## About the Book: What You'll Find Here

This book is divided into four parts.

In part one, "Setting the Foundation: Background and Development of Multidimensional Integrative Healing," you will learn about all the elements that came together to create Multidimensional Integrative Healing.

In part two, "Accessing the Resources of Multidimensional Integrative Healing," I outline ways to tap into foundational resources, along with spiritual, natural, and ancestral resources that can support you in many ways.

In part three, "Developing Energetic Sovereignty," I describe easy-to-learn practices for establishing healthy boundaries, grounding, connecting with your True Self, and controlling the exchange of energy through energetic cords.

Finally, in part four, "Dimensions of Spirit Work," I describe ways to work with dreams and enable after-death communication with EMDR. Finally, you will learn means to assess and recognize spirit attachments and strategies for facilitating spirit release.

## Conventions Used Throughout This Book

I have used fictitious first names for clients throughout the book. (I prefer the term *client* to *patient*.) All identifying details of cases have been changed to protect clients' privacy. I have changed names, professions, family constellations, races, and specific life events. Some cases represent composites of more than one client. All clients are referred to by first names, which I feel creates a more personal feeling about the people whose lives I describe. Some case examples in the book are my clients; others are clients of my EMDR colleagues.

In sections about particular cases where EMDR sessions are being described, a device using handheld vibrating pulsars or alternate tapping on the hands or knees may have been used.

This book is meant to be read sequentially, as many of the concepts and practices build on the ones that came before. At the back of the book you will find a listing of all the practices presented so that you can more easily access them. This book is meant for all who wish to expand ways of healing beyond the conventional psychotherapeutic context that relies on constructs that may constrain us. Many of the practices can be used by everyone, while some are meant for psychotherapists or healers to use with those they are helping. It is my greatest wish that this book expands your ways of thinking and working in a way that is multidimensional and healing for yourself and others you may work with.

# PART ONE

# Setting the Foundation

## *Background and Development of Multidimensional Integrative Healing*

Part one describes the story of how Multidimensional Integrative Healing (MDIH) was developed, my history and spiritual biography, and the terrible trauma that led me to creating MDIH from new ways I learned to heal myself and those I work with.

1

# Spiritual Influences and Teachers

The development of Multidimensional Integrative Healing (MDIH) arises out of my personal story, most importantly the spiritual teachers, teachings, and insights I have experienced over my life. The evolution of my thinking has occurred as a result of over fifty years of meditation practice and the understanding that has unfolded as the insights have been integrated into my life and work.

## Beginnings

All my life I have questioned things. As a child I was not content to accept what adults told me without asking for explanations I could understand. I rejected Christianity after my mother could not explain what the words to the Lord's Prayer meant and she expected me to accept Christian beliefs that made no sense to me. Then, when I was eight years old and President John F. Kennedy was assassinated, I became obsessed with and terrified of death.

What was death? What happened when we died? Because I found no comfort from the adults in my life, I turned inward and began to terrify myself before bed at night with thoughts of death. All I could think was that the death of the physical body was the end of life. That left me with the dreadful notion of the great void. Night after night I was filled with fear I tried my best to manage. Ultimately, in order to control my terror and be able to sleep, I decided to lock these thoughts away, to put the question of death in a box to be retrieved when I could find some answers.

I was finally able to open that box when in my junior year in high school I took a class titled "The Religious Impulse," which introduced me to the work of Alan Watts, Carlos Castaneda, Ram Dass, Aldous Huxley, Lama Govinda, and others. This course would start me on a path to finding answers to my deepest questions. I was especially drawn to the teachings of the Buddha that directed us to look within our own minds and to not believe without inquiry. This was liberating to me, and furthermore there were meditations and practices that aided me in finding answers from direct experience. I began a daily meditation practice and attended my first Tibetan Buddhist retreat when I was eighteen.

## Spiritual Teachers and Meditation Practices

Over the years I've had many spiritual influences that came together in the development of Multidimensional Integrative Healing. These include Tibetan Buddhism and my teacher Lama Thubten Yeshe, vipassana meditation as taught by Jack Kornfield and Joseph Goldstein, Advaita Vedanta nondualism and my teacher Jean Klein, and my spiritual friend and mentor Suzanne Segal.

### Lama Thubten Yeshe

In 1975, when I was twenty and a junior at Occidental College, I met my teacher Lama Thubten Yeshe and attended a three-week retreat with him and his disciple Lama Zopa in Lake Arrowhead, California. The intensive retreat in the mountains with Lama Yeshe was powerful and life-changing, especially the experience of being in Lama Yeshe's presence. When he entered the meditation hall bowing—hands together, radiant smile, sparkling eyes—he electrified the space as if we had been sitting in the dark and now a great light was shining. Blissful energy coursed through us, and our minds stilled. We were filled with this presence of great love and so much joy. He was also a living example of a person without an ego. He was fully himself: unselfconscious and compassionate.

During the first retreat and many times over the years, I was fortunate to be granted private meetings with him. In that first meeting, I discussed with him some things that were troubling me. At the end of the meeting, he gazed into my eyes and placed a hand on the top of my head and told me that I was "purified." In that moment I felt a surge of energy and light course through my entire body from the top of my head through all the cells of my body like being connected to a circuit of pure love. My mind stopped and tears streamed down my face. I had never experienced such love before. I recognize this now as what Lama called "Big Love." This also represented my initiation into the Buddha Dharma and a direct experience of what is beyond the ego or personal self.

Five years later, after another retreat and ceremony with Lama Yeshe, I told him how much I loved and appreciated him. He took my hand in his and covered my heart. Looking directly into my eyes, he said in a penetrating but tender tone, "The Buddha is within you, dear." His words struck me to my core. In an instant I recognized the truth of what he had said. My mind emptied. I felt in that moment the most powerful energy course through my body. Pure love. It was a transmission of love and an acknowledgment of my True Nature, which was not separate from his. This profound realization—that the teacher and the student are not separate, that we are the Buddha—frees the student from the teacher. This understanding is another basic principle of Multidimensional Integrative Healing. Enlightened wisdom—the Buddha—resides in us all. Our work is to help those with whom we work realize this.

Over the years I had the opportunity to receive many teachings and initiations into several Tibetan deities, including Avalokiteshvara (thousand-armed Buddha of compassion), Green Tara (female Buddha of compassion in action), Vajrapani (fearsome Buddha of power and protection), and Vajrasattva (Buddha of purification). During these powerful ceremonies, Lama would chant mantras, ring a prayer bell, move his hands in a dance of mudra, and enter deep meditative states invoking the deity he was initiating us into. After embodying the deity, he would ritually transfer that energy into each of us. I believe that these initiations into these deities with Lama Yeshe has had a deeper impact on my life than I realized at the time. They are in me, and the energy I experienced as he chanted and placed his hand on my head during the transmissions went deeper than I could have known. I have felt special affinity for Green Tara, female Buddha of compassion in action. The resource work we do in Attachment-Focused EMDR, as well as Multidimensional Integrative Healing, where we imagine and evoke spiritual helpers, is partially inspired by my lived experience.

## Vipassana Meditation

In 1976 I was introduced to vipassana meditation. My first eight-day silent retreat was taught by Joseph Goldstein and Sharon Salzberg in Washington state. I loved the practice of full days of sitting and walking meditation. The meditation consisted of finding your breath and then watching it dispassionately, making the mental note "in and out." When the mind is taken with a thought, you simply note that thinking is occurring and return to your breath. The same is done with body sensations or emotions. They are noted, and then you return your attention to your breath. This practice helps cultivate concentration, presence, a witness awareness, and disidentification with the mind-body process. We experience directly that who we are is not the body, senses, or mind. I was drawn to the simplicity of the meditation and the results I was experiencing of my mind quieting and insights into the nature of the mind arising. I had found the complexity of the visualizations used in Tibetan Buddhist practice difficult and complicated. A few months later I attended another eight-day retreat at the Lama Institute near Taos, New Mexico, taught by Jack Kornfield. Vipassana became my primary practice for years, and Jack became an important and beloved mentor.

The practice of dispassionately noting mind-body phenomena, the development of concentration and presence, is very important for all areas of our lives. It teaches us to quiet our minds, listen deeply, and notice what we are experiencing. These abilities are foundational to all healing we do for ourselves and others and essential to inner exploration of other dimensions.

Over the years during retreats, my meditation deepened, my mind dropped away, and I would sit for hours in stillness. I began to directly experience the teachings of the Buddha through the practice itself. Silence was the background out of which thoughts bubbled up, like from the bottom of a pond, with no self that was creating them. Just thoughts, just feelings, just body sensations. All discrete and unattached to a person.

Then one day in 1988 at a retreat in Santa Rosa, California, led by Jack, the ground disappeared along with any "me." Suddenly there was only consciousness, and everything arose out of it and was made of it at the same time. It was what I refer to as an inside-out moment—I was an extension of consciousness rather than experiencing it from an "I" position. I disappeared into the vastness of consciousness itself. This dissolution of a sense of a personal self lasted for several minutes, though I have no idea how long, as time disappeared. When I came back to "myself," I realized something profound had just happened, but I didn't have words for it.

In meeting with Jack later that day, I tried to convey what had happened. He asked me a series of questions, but I had few words to describe or explain. Yet the idea of practice no longer made any sense to me. The spiritual path had disappeared. How could there be a path when there is only this moment? I saw it as a construct, a thought like any other, and all constructs had lost meaning. Returning to my life postretreat was very difficult for me, as I felt disoriented. Jack began to mentor me, advising me by phone how to best manage the difficult transition. His compassionate guidance was deeply appreciated.

## Jean Klein and Nondual Spirituality

Not long after that retreat, when the spiritual path disappeared, I met Jean Klein. Jean helped put words and context to what had happened to me and opened me to a deeper understanding of our True Nature. Jean Klein was a European medical doctor, musicologist, and spiritual teacher (though he would never refer to himself as such) of Advaita Vedanta (nondualism). From Bohemia, he was in his late seventies with a formal, gentlemanly demeanor. When I attended a retreat he gave at the Mount Madonna Center in Watsonville, California, I was taken by the silence experienced in his presence. The more I sat with him, the more I dropped into the silence that felt like home. His words spoke directly to my experience and pointed to silence—to that which always is. Though he was not Buddhist, the teaching was in alignment with the most profound of the Buddhist teachings—that of no self, primordial presence, ground of being.

Jean Klein's retreats were not silent like the vipassana retreats that I was familiar with. They consisted of dialogues and hours-long sessions of body-sensing yoga. Jean drew his teaching from Advaita

Vedanta nondualism as well as from yogic practices from Kashmiri Shaivism. His body-sensing yoga taught me awareness of what he called "the energy body" and to deeply attune to the subtle sensations in my body. This nondual understanding and body sensing are integral aspects of Multidimensional Integrative Healing.

## Suzanne Segal

Another important teacher for me was Suzanne Segal. Suzanne was a clinical psychologist who some years before had the experience of the sense of a personal "I" spontaneously disappearing. After ten years of feeling unmoored and fearful, not understanding what had happened to her, she was introduced to Jean Klein, who provided context, validation, and guidance. As a result of his help, she entered what she called the "springtime" and was luminous, playful, and free. She began to meet with a group of us fellow psychotherapists and to teach from her understanding. I met with her in a group setting as well as individually every week over a period of six months. This intensive mentorship transformed my life.

Suzanne put words to the experiences I had had at the retreats and with Jean Klein. "Everything is the vastness and is an expression of the vastness. We are all made of the same substance," she told us. She spoke of the mind-body circuitry that has no self behind it. These patterns create identifications that we call "me" or "I" but have no substance. There was no judgment about any of the circuitry or the emotions that were included in the patterns. Regarding emotions, she would say dispassionately, "Fear is there too." None of the emotions that arise are any indication of the presence or absence of vastness.

Suzanne invited us to join her in knowing what was obvious and ever present. This vastness was felt and known in her presence. She removed all "specialness" around realization, as it is always in everything and everyone, our natural state. The group of psychotherapists who met with her—many of them Buddhists or students of nondualism—experienced an acceleration in our integration and realization of this abiding consciousness. Suzanne wrote a book about her experiences of awakening, *Collision with the Infinite*, that is a helpful guide and a gift to all. Suzanne wrote, "When asked who I am, the only answer possible is: I am the infinite, the vastness that is the substance of all things. I am no one and everyone, nothing and everything—just as you are."[1]

## Summary

### *Recognizing the Buddha Within Us*

Every one of my teachers emphasized that we are already the Buddha, and wisdom resides in each of us. The role of the teacher is to help the student know themself and access their inner teacher. All have been loving and deeply compassionate, essential qualities for a true teacher and spiritual guide. The practices they taught point us to realization rather than beliefs that we must accept. These fundamental values are intrinsic to the orientation we have in MDIH.

# 2

# EMDR and Its Evolution

Eye Movement Desensitization and Reprocessing (EMDR) is another important element of Multidimensional Integrative Healing (MDIH). With the focus on life-limiting memories and unhealthy patterns that are rapidly processed with bilateral stimulation, EMDR allows for clearing the past from our minds and bodies as well as integrating what is healthy and beneficial. I was introduced to EMDR by a psychologist friend in 1991. She raved about the amazing results she was achieving with her clients. Soon after this introduction, I attended a training by its developer, the psychologist Francine Shapiro, in Santa Clara, California. At that time, I was already an experienced clinical psychologist, having earned my doctorate in 1983, and was working in the San Francisco Bay Area specializing in the treatment of adults with childhood trauma.

At the training, Francine Shapiro presented the theoretical underpinnings for EMDR, the research findings to date, and explanation of the EMDR procedure. The framework for EMDR was cognitive-behavioral, yet the free-associative processing aspect was more like psychodynamic and Jungian therapies. The practicum part of the training was life-changing. All the EMDR trainings then and now require practice of the therapy being taught. During my first practice session, I chose an old memory from elementary school that I didn't deem very disturbing. Almost as soon as the therapist in the practice began to direct my eyes to track horizontally back and forth, I dropped back into a traumatic early-childhood memory involving my father. Yet instead of being stuck in this upsetting scene, with the eye movements continuing and the direction to "let whatever happens happen without censoring it," I maintained a dual focus of awareness and the disturbance in the memory cleared out of my system. It was as if I were in the scene and watching it at the same time.

As I rode the waves of strong emotions, I felt myself to be that frightened child, yet I was also dispassionately watching the scene unfold and the emotional charge dissipate like fog on a sunny day. By the end of the session, the disturbance in the memory had left and I had a global, objective view of what had occurred. I was very impressed with the power of this therapy. Not only was I able to resolve a traumatic experience in one session that had been held in my mind and body for most of my life, but it changed the interpersonal dynamic I had with my father at that time. I no longer carried a fear of him that I had since my childhood. I was able to experience him as an adult, with an adult-to-adult relationship that was contemporary.

EMDR incorporates alternating bilateral stimulation into a structured therapy. In the early days of EMDR, we were only using eye movements as the driver for the accelerated processing. But we found that other forms of alternating bilateral stimulation, such as tapping on either side of the body or sounds that shift bilaterally, work just as well. With EMDR we activate the memory network where the trauma is stored with the images, emotions, body sensations, and erroneous beliefs associated with it, and then we add bilateral stimulation. The bilateral stimulation that we use with EMDR activates an accelerated processing of the information that has been frozen in the nervous system. The processing that occurs with EMDR can be quite extraordinary and can look like active imagination in Jungian therapy. It is a mind-body free association with thoughts, feelings, old memories, or dreamlike fantasies that move rapidly through awareness. As this information is processed, new insights and new perspectives arise in the client. By the end of an EMDR session, the old memories no longer feel disturbing. You naturally arrive at a place of health and wholeness.

The fundamental theoretical model underlying EMDR is that of adaptive information processing. Shapiro discovered that when a trauma memory is activated and bilateral stimulation is applied within the structure of an EMDR session, we naturally move toward health and wholeness. She likened this to the natural healing system we have in our bodies that allows us to heal wounds after injury. The role of the therapist in EMDR is to facilitate this natural healing and to trust this capacity within the client. We don't add anything. We align with the healing potential within the client and only intervene if the processing is blocked in some way. I found this theory not only helpful in guiding the work but in alignment with the teachings from Lama Yeshe (the Buddha within) and Jean Klein.

Unpleasant experiences can create life-limiting memory networks. These networks can dramatically affect how we view ourselves and our world in the present because we create a sense of self from our interpretations of experiences. Jean taught that the ego is a contraction in the mind and body. Because these patterns are linked to feelings, they are experienced as "real" and define who we are. What I found to be so powerful—and in alignment with nondual teachings—was that when these patterns could be identified and the origins located from early experiences, EMDR processing could then "target" these experiences and reprocess them. When these old patterns of self-beliefs were processed with EMDR, they would dissolve, the restrictions in the mind and body would be liberated, and the person would feel free from the old patterns. In fact, clients would report elation, a release of energy that had been stuck, and deep insight that the old pattern did not define them: "Who I am is not defined by what happened to me."

## EMDR as a Transpersonal Psychotherapy

Years ago, Ram Dass criticized psychotherapy as simply rearranging the furniture of the ego. There was no real liberation from the old self-constructs. What I find with EMDR, in contrast, is that the furniture is removed from the room, and there is a feeling of spaciousness and disidentification from the old way of viewing oneself that is obvious and effortless. EMDR seems to clear the energetic, physical-emotional, and mental contractions from the mind and body, which deconstructs the self, providing us glimpses of freedom.

I believe that what we can facilitate with EMDR is to help our clients uncover their True Nature. Buddhism teaches that we are essentially whole. Lama Yeshe would say, "You are already enlightened." Wholeness is our True Nature. There is an abiding presence that is never touched by what happens to us. Like the sun obscured by clouds, it remains shining in the background. Upsetting life events and our interpretations of these events are like the clouds that obstruct our experience of our wholeness, our True Nature.

EMDR seems to clear the clouds from the sun. When these clouds are cleared at the end of a completed EMDR session, we experience an expression of this wholeness: wisdom, compassion, equanimity, power, and joy.

Within each of us is the potential to realize wholeness. This is another hallmark of EMDR's underlying Adaptive Informational Processing (AIP) model. We have a natural capacity for healing and a drive toward wholeness. This drive toward health, wholeness, and freedom comes from our highest source. Deep within us is the desire to be free from the constraints of identification with the false self. At the end of an EMDR session, when the burden of old constructs that have been abiding in our body-mind are released, we recognize as obvious that none of that defined us. We are not our conditioning.

We typically identify ourselves as the self-constructs that were developed through life experiences. We interpret these experiences as meaning something about who we are essentially. These experiences and their interpretations become encoded in the circuitry of our memory networks. We believe this circuitry is who we are, and we become imprisoned by our misconceptions. EMDR removes what is dysfunctional, maladaptive, and untrue, leaving in its wake an experience of freedom inherent in each human being. Who we are is this freedom, our ground of being ever present, luminous beingness. The natural expression of our being is love, compassion, joy, power, wisdom, peace, and creative expression. With EMDR we can focus our work on the blocks to our full expression. As the result of processing these, we experience our pure presence.

In addition to clearing the clouds of conditioning and experiencing spiritual freedom, many people have had varieties of spiritual/transpersonal experiences. These have included psychic experiences that transcend space and time, deep self-awareness, mysticism, epiphanies, spiritual insights, profound experiences of love and compassion for self and others, forgiveness, dramatic energy releases, experiences of bliss and sensory enhancement, experiences of peace and equanimity, a deep sense of well-being, contact with spiritual beings, contact with ancestors, past-life memories, and after-death communications.

Some of the experiences that people have reported during EMDR processing of traumas resemble those from shamanic practices such as spirit or soul retrieval, after-death communications, and contact with animal and ancestral spirits. These experiences have come to people who have not had any prior religious or spiritual interest or inclination, as well as to those who have in the past been spiritually oriented. I suspect that the bilateral stimulation used in EMDR not only clears that which isn't True Self but also opens us to altered states of consciousness. Ancient traditions around the world use drumming, rattling, and dancing as means of healing and connection with other dimensions of reality. These practices that use bilateral stimulation may lift the veil between worlds and invite energies from other dimensions that can aid in healing. I'll return to some of these ideas later.

I was so taken by the spiritual and transpersonal experiences my clients were having in the early days of my practice of EMDR that I began to take note of them. In 1996, I wrote about them in "Eye Movement Desensitization and Reprocessing (EMDR) and Spiritual Unfolding," an article for *The Journal of Transpersonal Psychology*

After completing my training in 1991, I began to use EMDR extensively in my clinical practice, achieving excellent results with my clients, many of whom had significant life-debilitating childhood traumas. I became a facilitator for the trainings and then a specialty presenter working with Francine Shapiro's EMDR Institute. In 1995 I began to teach EMDR through a doctoral program at California Institute for Integral Studies in San Francisco. One of my students from my EMDR course at California Institute for Integral Studies based his doctoral dissertation on my article and found that one of the most common experiences EMDR therapists reported their clients having was compassion for self and others following the completion of EMDR therapy. In 1997 I wrote my first book, *Transforming Trauma: EMDR,* which included clients' spiritual/transpersonal experiences.

## The Evolution of EMDR to Attachment-Focused EMDR

Since my EMDR training in 1991, I found the need to adapt the standard EMDR protocol as taught by Francine Shapiro and her institute according to the unique presentation of each person I see. At the time of the training, I was already an experienced psychologist, having been practicing for a decade already. I have always worked with complex trauma, as well as with people from diverse cultures and backgrounds. My early clinical work was in community mental health clinics working with a Spanish-speaking population. Many of the clients I have worked with experienced severe childhood sexual and physical abuse. I found early on that I needed to adjust the standard EMDR protocol for these clients to make it more relational, to help it flow better, and to increase safety. Clients needed additional work to strengthen and develop resilience before engaging in the often emotionally intense processing of traumatic memories.

One of the modifications I made to EMDR was to increase the use of what we call Resource Tapping. The resource work we do in Attachment-Focused EMDR, as well as Multidimensional Integrative Healing, is partially inspired by my lived experience. Resource Tapping is a modern psychospiritual method that echoes the spiritual technology of Tibetan Buddhist and other meditative traditions and is also influenced by hypnotherapy, guided imagery, positive psychology, and EMDR. Tibetan Buddhism in particular has developed highly sophisticated technologies for developing and cultivating different states of consciousness. Resource Tapping is a method of combining imagination with bilateral stimulation to link resources that are strengthening and beneficial to the person with their fuller neurocircuitry. Resource Tapping is not only used to provide support for clients, preparing them for the trauma processing part of EMDR, but also as a stand-alone technique that anyone can use.

Tapping in resources is related to EMDR but is an essentially different model. With EMDR we focus on the trauma memory, add bilateral stimulation, and follow a protocol that allows the unfolding of a free-associative processing. In contrast, when we tap in resources, we focus on the positive resource and only allow a short amount of bilateral stimulation. We keep the work focused exclusively on the positive, healing resources and do not allow a free flow of processing. Tapping in resources has been helpful for many people. It has become a wonderful tool that people are able to use to reduce anxiety, cope with trauma and illnesses, sleep better, and have increased confidence, among other things. Over time, a wealth of applications for tapping in resources has been developed. I wrote about ways to use Resource Tapping in my books *Tapping In*, *Rewiring the Addicted Brain with EMDR-Based Treatment*, and *Attachment-Focused EMDR: Healing Relational Trauma*.

We use resources in Attachment-Focused EMDR in many ways to help in healing. We use them to help strengthen the client prior to trauma-processing work, to help when processing becomes blocked, and to repair developmental deficits by creating in imagination what the client needs to grow in a healthy way. In preparing for trauma processing, we tap in resources from four main categories that we refer to as the Four Foundational Resources. These are Peaceful Place, Nurturing Figures, Protector Figures, and Wise Figures.

Attachment-Focused EMDR is an orientation to the practice of EMDR. AF-EMDR is client-centered and emphasizes a reparative therapeutic relationship using a combination of Resource Tapping to strengthen clients, EMDR to process traumas, and talk therapy to help integrate the information from EMDR sessions and to provide healing derived from therapist-client interactions. AF-EMDR can be used for clients with severe early-attachment trauma, as well as for all clients who require that the therapist attend to their needs as unique individuals.

In 2016 I established the Parnell Institute for Attachment-Focused EMDR through which our team of educators provides trainings, workshops, and a process for certification for therapists trained in this way of healing. In this book I will be referring to EMDR as well as Attachment-Focused EMDR in the cases presented.

# 3

# Multicultural Experience

An important contributor to Multidimensional Integrative Healing is a cross-cultural perspective that is open and accepting of many ways of viewing life. My experiences living, traveling, and working with people from around the world have contributed to my expanded awareness and conviction of the importance of this perspective to healing.

I have had a love of travel and diverse cultures since I was in my teens. I was fourteen years old when I learned to speak Spanish in a summer language immersion course and our family took a road trip to Baja California. The Mexicans I met were open and friendly, greeting me with a smile and a "Buenos días. ¿Cómo estás?" I began to speak in Spanish with ease because the people I met encouraged my efforts to connect with them in their language.

When I was sixteen, I joined Amigos de las Americas, an organization that trained teens in basic first aid as well as how to set up a medical clinic and administer vaccinations. After weeks of training I was placed with another teen girl in a small village in the highlands of Guatemala, where we created a clinic for the local population of Kiche people. With the village as our base, we vaccinated fourteen hundred people, often venturing into the small villages with a local man who could interpret Spanish and the local Kiche dialect. My friend and I slept on cots in a simple cement-block hut with a dirt floor. Two local women with their babies wrapped in brightly colored cloth prepared our meals over an open fire. I adored the people of the village where I lived. There was a peacefulness in that village. The people were kind and generous and seemed to live in harmony with their surroundings. During this time, the people who came to the clinic seemed to have enough food and adequate shelter, and I did not observe the malnutrition and serious illnesses among the population I saw the following year when I lived in Colombia, a seemingly more affluent country. I believe it is important to note that I was in Guatemala in 1971, before the genocide of the Mayan people that devastated the region from 1975 until the first half of the 1980s. After my experience in the highlands of Guatemala I determined to become a medical doctor so that I could travel and help people in different parts of the world.

In the summer of 1972 Amigos de las Americas placed me and another teen girl in Armenia, Colombia. This was completely different from what I had experienced in Guatemala. We were housed in a hospital and ventured door to door with local nurses to vaccinate the local children for polio. Though seemingly more affluent and modern than Guatemala, what I saw in the homes of the people was horrifying. Children with bloated bellies and spindly arms and legs were starving. Some had old men's faces on tiny, emaciated bodies. In the hospital, babies screamed in the night as nurses struggled to get nourishment into them. I learned that the problem in this part of Colombia was that the fertile land was planted with coffee and bananas that were grown for export, leaving little room to grow crops to feed the community.

During college in Los Angeles, I volunteered as a Spanish interpreter at the general hospital and had exposure to the plight of immigrants and their health issues. One summer I lived in southern Mexico in San Cristóbal de las Casas, studying anthropology and living with a local family.

In my twenties I married a Spanish-speaking immigrant. He was a highly educated civil engineer, but his education and licensure were not accepted in the United States. He struggled to learn English—his third language—find work, and adapt to a foreign culture. As a result, he suffered from mental health challenges that ultimately took a toll on our marriage.

I have always worked with people from cultures that differ from my own. I find that this exposure expands my perspective on life. I think about things differently and approach therapy with an open, curious mind. For many years I worked in community mental health clinics that served low-income clients who were primarily Spanish-speaking, African American, and from many other cultural backgrounds. I witnessed firsthand how oppressed communities face different mental health challenges as they have to navigate a hostile environment and society on top of their own personal struggles.

Adding to the multicultural perspective I bring to the development of MDIH is my extensive travel experience. Over the years I have traveled to forty-four countries for work and leisure. For twenty-one years I have lived part-time in northern Mexico, where I have learned firsthand how corruption and violence keep a people from prospering and feeling safe. These experiences have educated me about present-day issues and history from the perspective of the people who live in these different regions. It has also provided an expanded awareness and appreciation of the narrowness of the view I carry from my own culture, which is influenced by growing up in the San Francisco Bay Area.

## My Introduction to Indigenous Practices and Their Impact on Multidimensional Integrative Healing

Over the years I have had the privilege to have participated in rituals and ceremonies conducted by Tibetan Buddhist teachers as well as Indigenous elders and shamans from the sacred valley of the Peruvian Andes and the Peruvian Amazon, the Ecuadorian Andes and Sapara and Achuar people from the sacred headwaters of the Amazon in Ecuador, a Lakota elder, Pyramid Lake Paiute people, and others. Though I was not raised Buddhist, and Tibet was not my home or culture, the pujas performed by the lamas with chanting, incense, and bell ringing felt familiar to me, evoking a deep sense of homecoming, a yearning to lose myself in timelessness. A significant event linking Tibetan and Native American ceremony took place by a sacred lake in Nevada.

## Lama Yeshe and Paiute Ceremony to Protect a Sacred Lake

In 1980, during a break in a retreat that Lama Yeshe was giving in the Sierras, I was invited by a friend and fellow Dharma student to drive Lama Yeshe to Pyramid Lake. The purpose was to join a group of Native Americans to do a puja ceremony with Lama to protect the lake, which was drying up because of development taking the water.

Pyramid Lake is a high desert lake covering 125,000 acres. One of the largest natural lakes in Nevada, it is sacred to the Northern Paiute people, who have lived on its shores for thousands of years. Like a magnificent mirror, the water changes color from shades of blue to gray depending on the formation of the clouds above. Arriving at this spectacular lake, we were met by a small group of Pyramid Lake Paiute people who were to join us in the puja to preserve the lake. Lama told us that the lake reminded him of a lake in Tibet where people went to gaze into the mirrorlike surface for meditation and divination. After greeting our hosts, Lama quickly put us to work gathering tinder to build a fire. I don't remember much about what we did except that we sat cross-legged around the small fire while Lama chanted and occasionally added things he had with him into the flames. Before the ceremony, we were laughing and joking around with Lama, but when he began, he became serious and focused. When he began puja, clouds hovered above us, but when he began to chant, the clouds parted right above him. As soon as the puja was over, the clouds returned and a flock of magnificent white pelicans flew in from the north, sweeping over us before taking off into the sky like a blessing.

For the Paiute, the ceremony Lama Yeshe conducted was familiar. It was much like ceremonies they did. This link between cultures seemed to erase the geographic separation between Tibet in far East Asia and the Paiute in the West. We sat together in a circle around the small fire, Lama chanting in his deep, resonant voice. As he intoned words to invoke energies that would protect the sacred lake, we dropped into a place that was timeless and well known.

This introduction to Paiute and Tibetan rituals would add to my familiarity and comfort with rituals and ceremonies I have participated in over the years, as well as my deep appreciation for the power of these practices. The more I learn about rituals that are nature-based and performed in cultures found in regions in many parts of the world, the more I realize their universality. Similar practices were performed in Europe before the arrival of Christianity and their prohibition. Some of the practices I have been introduced to by various teachers have contributed to the development of MDIH.

## My Introduction to Shamanism

My teacher and friend Suzanne Segal eventually learned she had been diagnosed with a brain tumor. As she lay in a coma, I spent several hours at her bedside in her home in Stinson Beach. Her long brown hair had been shaved, and she had a large scar on the side of her head in the shape of a question mark. I meditated for hours sitting by her bedside, sending her all the love in my heart. It was a sacred time of deep peace. I felt like I journeyed far away, but there was so much love.

After my time sitting with Suzanne as she was dying, I had trouble functioning. It was as if the psychic energetic barrier between me and others had disappeared. In sessions with my clients, I knew what they were feeling and what they were going to say before they said it. There was no separation between us. It was like I had no skin. I was raw and completely open in a way that made me permeable to everything around me. I suspected that I had lost a part of myself when I sat with Suzanne in meditation. I knew I needed help.

I had a good friend I could turn to who would understand and might be able to help me. She was a psychologist who was engaged in a yearslong study of neo-shamanism with Michael Harner and Sandra Ingerman. She determined that what had happened to me was a soul loss. She offered to work with me to help retrieve it using techniques she had learned. I don't recall what was done except that she used rattling as she journeyed to help with the retrieval of what had left me. As a result of our session, I returned to feeling in my body and my psychic energetic boundaries returned.

Through my friend and sharing experiences, I learned to some degree about shamanism. From time to time she would do a journey for me to bring back information that she felt would be useful for me. I never knew if what she conveyed to me was true or not, as it came from her. Instinctively I did not trust the neo-shamanism that contemporary instructors were teaching because it was not based in service, healing, or the empowerment of the person the practitioner was helping. The shaman did the work, and the person they were helping was a passive receiver of the information that the shaman brought back to them. The shaman held all the power.

Over the years I have known people who have studied with shamans with mixed results. Some shamans are focused on the development of power, accumulating student adherents, and making money. I could see that the accumulation of power without compassion could be dangerous. This view was supported by EMDR work I did with a woman who had been terribly traumatized by shamans in South America. The same ego inflation and struggle for power were going on in the shamanic world with curses being sent from one shaman to another.

However, my friend introduced me to many of the concepts that allowed me to recognize when a client I was working with in an EMDR session had spirit or soul loss. But instead of me doing the work to retrieve it, I found ways that clients could do it themselves through inquiry and resources that they chose.

# 4

# My Son's Death and My Healing Journey

On April 11, 2020, my life changed forever in a terrible and traumatic way that broke me apart. On Sunday, April 26, 2020, after searching for my forty-one-year-old son for two weeks, including the use of a private investigator and multiple police departments, I was informed that he had been found murdered in his San Francisco apartment. Upon learning that my worst fears had come true, over the phone from the private investigator, I entered nowness, knowing without words that everything was and is exactly as it should be. I knew without argument that all is perfect as it is in all the terribleness, horror, and grief. Stillness, love, just this. I dropped into the isness of this. Later the pain came—gut-wrenching pain.

What has unfolded for me over the last several years has been a journey of healing and learning, opening to new dimensions that I had known about but had not understood how to navigate or work with.

Soon after learning of my son's murder, we began to receive communications from him from the other side. These were coming through dreams and visits he was making with friends and family members. His former girlfriend began to channel communications from him that he seemed to want passed on to his loved ones, though she had never had such experiences. These were for the most part ecstatic, joyful, and loving. My mother felt his presence near her. I was having dreams of trying to put the pieces together. I was concerned that he wasn't okay. I had learned from Tibetans that how you die is important, and I believed that a bad death, like he had, required help. I felt compelled to find help for him. I put the word out to my community that I needed a shaman healer who could help heal me, my family, and my son who had been killed. I sought someone who could clear the space where his life was taken, clear the dark energy around what happened to him, help him ascend to the light, and clear anything that was holding him. I also wanted someone who could help me move through the overwhelm and grief so that I could be of service to others.

## Jean Schneider: Spirit Worker, Healer, and Mentor

My call for help brought the teacher, mentor, healer, and spirit worker Jean Schneider into my life. I felt an immediate connection and deep trust of Jean. She has a clear mind, an open heart, and no ego. Putting all her skills and experience to use, she was able to aid my son to cross over. She worked on clearing the energy and patterns that had led to the violent end of his life. After Jean completed her work, my dreams changed. I no longer sought to put pieces together.

Jean refers to herself as a spirit worker and uses practices she learned from her mentors and teachers. Her practices are nature-based and derive from multiple sources where the information was passed to her orally. For this reason, I cannot direct you to her sources, as she has learned from many different teachers from different countries and traditions, and their sources were passed down orally from their teachers.

After we felt my son had received the help he needed, I continued to work with Jean, at first to help with my healing and then to learn about ways to work with multiple dimensions to help others.

Early in my healing from grief that at times felt unsurvivable, Jean suggested that I give the trees my grief so that it could be accepted into the earth as compost. Sometimes that was insufficient, and I connected with a nearby mountain I loved that was old, large, and better able to absorb the enormity of my devastation. Time changed for me; a bigger view developed and a deeper knowing that physical death was not the end of life. Through Jean's mentoring I learned expanded ways of helping people, using spirit-work skills and understanding, as well as energy work, to empower the "client," not the practitioner. Through inquiry we help our clients find words for what they need and what to do next. In doing so, we strengthen their inner knowing and activate the natural healing capacity and wisdom inherent in them.

## Lifting the Clouds of Sadness with Manari Ushigua, a Sapara Shaman and Teacher

Despite the healing work with Jean and the EMDR I had done to clear the trauma, as well as the love and support from my family and friends, I continued to be burdened with sadness that would not lift. I was no longer experiencing the extreme grief I had in the early months, but sadness clouded everything. I could remember feeling happy, like a distant dream or from a past self, but I could not experience it. To heal and return to myself, I felt perhaps a connection with the natural world would help. I wanted to feel the interconnectedness of nature through an immersion, far from the civilized world, in a place where people lived in harmony with nature.

Years earlier, my husband and I had ventured into the Peruvian Amazon and experienced a deep connection with what felt like the heart of nature. I thought perhaps returning to this primordial natural world would help me feel the interconnectedness of life and support my healing. With that in mind, in January 2022, my husband and I joined a small group organized by Pachamama Journeys and traveled by small plane into the Sacred Headwaters of the Ecuadorian Amazon.

After a cleansing ceremony with a traditional healer woman in the Andes, we flew by small plane deep into the jungle, landing on a tiny strip of land that seemed to appear out of nowhere. There in the thick jungle we were greeted by a small group of Sapara people from the nearby village and led to a clearing by a river where we were again ceremonially cleansed with tobacco smoke and brushed with plant bundles. We were directed to sniff tobacco juice that burned our throats, gave us head rushes, and made our eyes tear up. Sapara women painted our faces with red and black plant-based paint. The shaman, Manari Ushigua, who wore a colorful feathered headdress and intricate beaded necklaces, greeted each of us and gave us each a Sapara name. He called me Shamina, "female shaman."

Manari is the spiritual and political leader of the Sapara Nation. He is a protector of the forest and a healer. I didn't know it at the time, but he teaches Indigenous wisdom, particularly around dreamwork, internationally and has a large following. He met with us in the circle to teach us about the importance of dreams. He encouraged us to remember our dreams and to report them to him when we met in the morning.

The following morning, when he asked us about our dreams, I recalled them as usual. Since I was a child, I have had recall of my dreams, and I am often lucid in my dreaming. My dreams the night before were fragmented and sad. I told him about the dreams, the tragic death of my son, and the sadness that was ever present. He indicated that he wanted to work with me privately during a break.

Manari guided me to a clearing by the river, where I sat on a tree stump. He stood facing me, then he made his way around me as he chanted, blew smoke on my head, and sprayed me with liquid from his mouth. Speaking to me in Spanish, he told me that my sadness was hurting my son. He told me to have the sadness rise like a cloud and then make rain that would replenish the earth. I experienced Manari's deep compassion wash over me as he did this ceremony. When he was done, I felt as though something had lifted. The cloud that had hung over me had vanished. He embraced me and told me that I was a wise teacher, a shaman, and I was powerful. My son was a protector for me. He was there with me.

Later that day, I found myself playing with an exuberant ten-year-old boy from the village. As we were led on a hike through the jungle, he stayed near me, climbing trees barefoot and stripping off leaves to weave a bracelet for me as well as a crown I placed upon my head for his admiration. We had a connection and a wordless affection for each other. He reminded me of my son when he was a boy—playful, adventurous, and good-hearted.

The healing Manari did for me was profound. The heaviness lifted and has not returned. I still feel sad, and at times I experience gut-wrenching grief, but the ever-abiding sadness has gone.

## Healing by the Sacred Kapok Tree

Later, during that journey in the Amazon, I had another healing experience. This one came from a deep sense of connection with a majestic ancient tree. Led by a vigorous elder shaman from the Achuar people, our group hiked several miles deep into the jungle to a sacred kapok tree. This enormous tree was a place where for hundreds of years the Achuar people performed ritual and ceremony. I circled the enormous tree, then I closed my eyes and placed my hands on her trunk and meditated. Communing with this tree, I felt connected to deep roots and branches that reached into the sky. The sense of timeless multidimensionality was evident. This was the tree of life that I have seen represented in cultures around the world. As my mind emptied, these words came to me:

Remember Me
to Grandmother Kapok Tree of the Amazon
Silent sentinel of the forest
Ancient
Deep roots connected to other roots
that sustain and support me
Your hair is the branches that reach for the sky
and the upper world of connections.
I am you and you are me
Remember me
I will bring you home to yourself
Rooted in now and connected to everything
In all directions
Merge with my spirit
I'll help you

The time in the Amazon immersed in nature with the Sapara and Achuar people, and the healing I experienced with Manari, indeed helped to lift the heaviness of the loss and link me more fully to our multidimensional interconnectedness and the dimensions of reality beyond the one we call "real." The connection with Indigenous cultures with traditions and practices unbroken for thousands of years was a reminder of what has been lost in our so-called modern world and what can be recovered.

## Summary

### *Setting Our Intention–Service and Healing, Ethical Boundaries, and Finding the Answers Within*

I understand now that when we have service and healing as intention in our work, an ethical structure, and clear boundaries, and we empower our clients to find the answers within, spirit work is simply an expanded skillful means of healing. All of this—all the tools and techniques we use for healing, whether in the material world or in other dimensions—is an expression of the same Consciousness. All of our methods and approaches are made of the same substance, arising out of vastness and disappearing into it. It is the same isness, the same illuminated nowness that animates all phenomena.

Since my son's death, after I received so much help from Jean Schneider, a group of dedicated and experienced AF-EMDR therapists have continued to learn from her. We are integrating EMDR work with what she has taught us about boundaries and energetic sovereignty, energetic cords, True Self, releasing spirit attachments, and more. From our experience working with these tools and sharing our discoveries, we have learned much that has helped to expand the way in which we are working, bringing healing to even more people. I have returned to Buddhism and the bodhisattva intention to relieve suffering in the world, but without identification as anyone or anything special or focus on a reward. I am taking what has been broken in me and finding a new form of healing that uses EMDR to process traumas and to integrate experiences and skills and techniques from spirit and energy work traditions to create a way of healing that is Multidimensional Integrative Healing.

# PART TWO

# Accessing the Resources of Multidimensional Integrative Healing

In part two you will learn Resource Tapping, a technique for strengthening and integrating supportive resources. You will be introduced to the Four Foundational Resources—Peaceful Place, Nurturing Figures, Protector Figures, and Wise Figures—and how they can be helpful to you in your life. Building on this foundation, you will learn about accessing and tapping in spiritual resources and resources from nature, as well as drawing from your ancestral lineage, to find a wealth of resources there. All of these resources can be tapped in and used to support you in many areas of your life.

# 5

# Your Four Foundational Resources

In the United States we have a "pull yourself up by your bootstraps" culture. We are praised for being self-reliant, and we are not comfortable asking for help. But there are times in all our lives when managing life challenges alone is too hard. During these times, we may be advised by caring people to "just be with it"—whatever "it" is—mindfully. But what if the feelings that are arising are too much for us to be with? What if we need more help? What if the situation we find ourselves confronting requires resources that are beyond our capacities?

Within each of us is a hidden potential, our untapped natural resources. We have inside everything we need for healing our psychological wounds. The problem is that these resources too often remain buried underground. We don't know how to access them. Many spiritual traditions teach ways to contact our resources by using prayer and meditation practices. Today in Western psychology we have found a powerful new way to harness the power of our untapped inner resources.

This chapter builds on and expands the information in my book *Tapping In*, providing an overview and step-by-step instructions for Resource Tapping. It describes the Four Foundational Resources we use in Attachment-Focused EMDR as well as others that support grounding, embodiment, and spiritual practice.

Over the years in my work as an EMDR therapist as well as in my personal life, I have learned that it is important to develop resources that can support us. These resources can help increase our capacity to manage challenges and emotional overwhelm and provide inner strength. Resources include people, places, images, qualities, memories, and experiences—real or imagined—that we can draw upon to develop resilience and help in healing. Resources may also include inherent qualities such as love, wisdom, and joy.

The practice of Resource Tapping (pairing an activated resource with bilateral stimulation) is one way to develop supportive resources. EMDR therapists have found that when we activate a desired resource with the image, feeling state, and any associated sensory information and then add short sets of alternating bilateral stimulation such as tapping on either shoulder or sides of the legs, drumming, or using auditory stimulation bilaterally, the activated resource is more fully linked into our neuro-network.

With Attachment-Focused EMDR we tap in Four Foundational Resources in the early part of treatment:

- Peaceful Place
- Nurturing Figures
- Protector Figures
- Wise Figures

These resources help to prepare clients for the trauma processing and provide information to the therapist about the inner strengths of the client. These foundational resources strengthen clients during sessions and provide support between sessions and in daily life. When a person has learned to tap in their resources, they can call them to mind and use them for managing anxiety, helping to sleep, deactivating triggers for substance use or abuse, and boosting performance. They are an excellent self-help tool with many clinical applications. Resource Tapping has become a stand-alone technique that you can make use of, even outside of EMDR therapy. Here is one such practice for you to try.

## PRACTICE: TAPPING IN RESOURCES

Tapping in resources can include many forms of alternating bilateral stimulation. You can tap on your legs or knees, like drumming. You can lift your feet and tap them on the floor or march in place. It is important to tap one side and then the other. In this way you stimulate each side of your brain. There are even devices that have been developed for this purpose that have pulsars you hold in your hands or place under your legs that vibrate alternately and headphones to provide auditory stimulation. You can use what is called the Butterfly Hug: You cross your arms over your chest and tap either shoulder. Another version of this is Eagle Wings Flapping, as described by First Nations elder and EMDR therapist Shelley Pompana Spear Chief.[1] For Native people from some tribes, the butterfly is not a symbol they would wish to use, as the butterfly has a short life and dies. The eagle for many tribes has a more positive connotation and is significant to their cultural traditions. With Eagle Wings Flapping, you hook your thumbs together at your heart with your two palms forming wings that can beat at your chest, creating rhythmic bilateral stimulation. Many Indigenous traditions around the world use drumming or rattling. Discover what works best for you.

### Steps for Tapping In Your Resources

These steps are the most basic approach to tapping in resources.

Close your eyes and go inside, bringing your attention to a quiet, still place inside yourself.

Call to mind the resource you have chosen to work with. It can be a positive memory, an inherent quality, an experience, or an important person or animal. Imagine the resource as well as you can. Open your senses. Pay special attention to how you feel in your body.

I want to note here that you do not have to have an ability to visualize well in order to gain benefit from this resourcing work. Many people do not "see," but they can imagine or get a strong sense of the resource they desire to activate. We desire the activation of the feeling state, the energetic signature of the resource that then enables that resource to be accessible to you.

When you have a strong sense of the resource, when you can feel its quality, begin to tap on your knees, right-left, right-left, or any kind of bilateral stimulation that you wish to employ. Tap six to twelve times, then stop and check in with yourself. If it feels good and the resource is strengthening, you can tap some more. You can continue to tap as long as it feels positive. If other memories or resources come to mind that feel good, you can tap them in also.

Begin to tap at a slow, rhythmic pace and then find the pace that feels best to you. While you tap, focus on the whole feeling the resource evokes, allowing the feeling to increase. At first you might tap for only a short time, approximately six to twelve times, right-left, right-left, then stop and check in with yourself. How was that for you? What were you experiencing? If the resource is strengthened, you can tap some more. You may continue tapping as long as it remains positive. Some people prefer longer rounds of tapping. This is fine as long as the resource remains positive.

If the resource should flip to the negative or become contaminated in some way (e.g., you remember your Peaceful Place was sold and you cannot go there anymore), you should stop the bilateral stimulation. You don't want to activate memory networks that are going to be distressing to you. Many people can only do a short amount of bilateral stimulation before they begin to commence free-associative processing that can take them far afield. It is best to do short sets and check in. Some people can tap much longer, and the resource gets stronger. You might even begin to recall a series of positive memories that strengthen the resource. If this happens, you can continue with bilateral stimulation.

If the resource has been contaminated and no longer feels positive, there are a few things you can try.

- After you have stopped bilateral stimulation, see if you can think of a different resource that is fully positive. It is important that the resource feel completely positive. If you can find another one, add bilateral stimulation, this time for a shorter duration.

- If a distressing memory has arisen, you can imagine placing it in a container that can hold it for you. This container can be made of anything you can imagine that can safely hold the material that has come up. When you feel the memory sufficiently contained, you can return to the resource you began with or bring up another one that has only positive feelings and associations. This time, tap for a very short time.

## The Four Foundational Resources

The Four Foundational Resources we use in Attachment-Focused EMDR comprise a basic tool kit that creates a structure upon which we can add many other resources. These resources can be easily summoned and tapped in for many kinds of problems or situations. Most people can access these resources. By locating and tapping in these resources before they are needed, you are consciously developing these most important and useful tools and placing them where they can be easily found.

### Peaceful Place

The Peaceful Place is a resource that can be developed and tapped in to create a sense of calm and to reduce anxiety. It is one of the resources used most often for this purpose. The Peaceful Place is a place where you feel relaxed and at ease. It can be a known place or an imaginary place. Many people choose a place in nature, such as a beautiful beach or mountain lake. It can also be symbolic, such as in the arms of a large mother bear or in a warm, cozy cottage that you create in your imagination. In developing the Peaceful Place, you want to create a place of self-nourishment and comfort where you can relax. For some people, the purpose of the Peaceful Place is to help them relax and feel secure; for others, the emphasis is more on it being a sanctuary where they can contact their wisdom and creativity. Alternatives to the Peaceful Place are Sacred Place or Sanctuary, Happy Place, Calm Place, and imagining engaging in a healthy activity that is enjoyable and uplifting. Some people imagine going to their Peaceful Place as a means of self-soothing and can even use it before going to sleep at night.

The Peaceful Place imagery has been described and used by many people. Simply imagining a place that is easeful and comfortable can be powerful in and of itself. However, combining imagination and bilateral stimulation serves to strengthen the imagery more fully by integrating it into the nervous system, making it more accessible. Many people have tapped in their Peaceful Places during times of stress to help create a feeling of calm. People in countries all over the world have used this resource with excellent results. You can enhance your resources by drawing or painting them. Afterward you can display your drawings where you can see them or even create a book of your resources that you can carry with you as a reminder of your Peaceful Place to help you recall it whenever you feel the need.

## PRACTICE: TAPPING IN A PEACEFUL PLACE

Close your eyes and go inside. Do deep, slow breathing or another breathing method to calm yourself and help you come to the present moment.

Now that you are relaxed, invite a place to come to mind where you feel peaceful and relaxed, a place where you feel comfortable and at ease. It can be a place you have been to before or that you create in your imagination. What is most important is that when you connect with this place, you feel a sense of ease and well-being.

If you need help connecting with it, you can enhance it using your senses:

What do you see?

What do you hear?

What do you smell?

What do you feel?

What sensations do you feel on your skin?

When you have a strong positive feeling of this place, and you feel relaxed and at ease, begin to tap, right-left, right-left, at a pace that feels comfortable to you. Continue to tap as long as it feels positive and continues to strengthen. Stop when you feel that it is well established.

If you feel distress or experience the intrusion of negative imagery, stop tapping immediately. For many people, the bilateral stimulation works quite well to increase the feeling and imagery more securely, but for some people, the bilateral stimulation opens up processing of distressing material. If this happens, stop tapping and explore what you are experiencing. You may need to develop a new Peaceful Place using imagery only or work to create changes in the Peaceful Place that make it secure.

## Nurturing Figures

Nurturing Figures are real or imaginary figures who have a compassionate, nurturing quality. The feeling state we desire to activate is one of a soothing, comforting presence. They are kind, caring, compassionate, and loving. They can include figures from the present or past, inner guides, and even animals. They can be people from the past who were loving, safe, nurturing figures in your life. There may be a parent or stepparent, sibling, grandparent, nanny, aunt or uncle, teacher, coach, doctor, counselor, friend's parent, or clergy person who was an important source of caring for you. There may be people from your current life who are important resources for you—a spouse, friend, or lover. Figures from movies, TV, books, history, or popular culture can be used as nurturing resources too. Spiritual figures such as Kwan Yin, Tara, Mary, Jesus, a wise elder, or an angel can be nurturers. Animals—pets from your present or past or animals for which you have a special affinity—can be valuable nurturing figures. Perhaps you have a dog or cat that comforts you, or you had a pet you loved in the past.

Many people have a spiritual connection with an animal or mythological creature (e.g., wolf, bear, lion, panther, elephant, owl, coyote, snake, eagle, or dragon). In many Indigenous spiritual traditions, these are animal allies or guides that carry a sacred quality. These animals can be imagined and tapped in and can serve as nurturers, protectors, and wisdom speakers.

I want to note, too, that Nurturing Figures do not have to be someone or something that provides nurturing to you. What is important here is that when the figure is imagined, it lights up the network of this resource and you feel it. Remember, the resource—whether real or a creation of your imagination—is all experienced within you.

I typically try to find more than one figure, as each one has a different feeling and fills a different need. For example, for Nurturing Figures, I call up my friend Joan, my spiritual teacher Lama Yeshe, and a beloved group of women friends.

## PRACTICE: TAPPING IN YOUR NURTURING FIGURES

You can begin by compiling a list of Nurturing Figures, then tap them in, one at a time. The following is a script for tapping in your Nurturing Figures.

Think of a figure or figures that you associate with nurturing. This figure is kind, caring, compassionate, and loving. This can be a real or imagined person, a spiritual figure, someone from a book or movie, or an animal. You don't have to imagine the Nurturing Figure providing nurturing to you. What is important is that the figure represents that quality and that you can feel it inside when you imagine them. Make a list of these figures.

Begin with the first one. Close your eyes and go inside, bringing up the image of the Nurturing Figure as strongly as you can. When you imagine the figure and have a strong sense of the nurturing quality of the figure, begin bilateral stimulation. (Use bilateral stimulation for six to twelve right-lefts. Then stop and check in with yourself. How was that for you? How do you feel?)

If the nurturing quality is continuing to strengthen, you can do more bilateral stimulation if you wish. Continue bilateral stimulation as long as you feel the figure and the nurturing quality strengthening and integrating.

If you have more than one resource, bring to mind the next Nurturing Figure and tap it in. Repeat this process, tapping in one resource at a time.

For example, imagine your compassionate angel. When you can feel her nurturing quality, begin to tap. When it feels complete—when you feel it more deeply, you then move on to the next Nurturing Figure on the list. For example, imagine your dog, Buddy, demonstrating his nurturing. When you have a good sense of that, begin to tap.

## Protector Figures

Protector Figures are figures real or imaginary that have a protective quality. Protector Figures can include people or animals, or imaginary figures from books, movies, TV, or dreams. It is most important that when the protector is imagined, you can feel the quality of protection the figure represents. Many people choose animals as protectors. They can include pets or even animals that have a spiritual or numinous feeling. One of my clients had a powerful panther ally who served as her protector, while another person chose a mother bear. Spiritual figures from many traditions can be used, including protective angels and deities. As in the case with the Nurturing Figures, you do not have to imagine yourself being protected. We are summoning the energy of the figure and tapping it in. Nurturing Figures and Protector Figures can be the same figures but manifest different energies. For example, a mother grizzly bear can be imagined cuddling her cubs as a nurturer and fiercely protecting them as the manifestation of protection.

### PRACTICE: TAPPING IN YOUR PROTECTOR FIGURES

Begin by compiling a list of Protector Figures; then tap them in, one at a time. The following is a script for tapping in your Protector Figures.

Think of a figure or figures that you associate with protection. It can be real or imaginary. It can be someone you know from the present or past, an animal, or even a figure from a movie, book, TV, or dreams. It can be a spiritual figure that is protective. It can be your adult protective self. You don't have to imagine the Protector Figure protecting you. What is important is that the figure represent that quality and that you can feel it inside when you imagine them. Make a list of these figures.

Begin with the first one. Close your eyes and go inside, bringing up the image of the Protector Figure as strongly as you can. When you imagine the figure and feel the protective quality in your body, begin bilateral stimulation. Use bilateral stimulation for six to twelve right-lefts, then stop and check in with yourself. How was that for you? How do you feel?

If the protective quality is continuing to strengthen, you can do more bilateral stimulation if you wish. Continue bilateral stimulation as long as you feel the figure and the protective quality strengthening and integrating.

If there is more than one resource, you can bring the next Protector Figure to mind and tap it in. Repeat this process, tapping in one resource at a time.

For example, imagine your mother grizzly bear protecting her cubs. When you can feel her protective quality, begin to tap. Tap as long as it feels good to you. Keep tapping until it feels complete. Then move on to the next Protective Figure on the list. For example, begin with the mother bear, tap her in; then imagine your best friend, John, demonstrating his protective quality, then tap that in.

## Wise Figures

The Wise Figure is associated with wisdom. When you think of a wise being, what comes up for you? Such Wise Figures can include people you have known personally, such as family members with whom you are close or people from your family you have never met but you've heard about. Wise Figures can also be spiritual figures, characters from movies or TV, literary characters, or historical figures. Some people have used Gandalf from *The Lord of the Rings* or Yoda from the *Star Wars* movies. Other Wise Figures to use as resources could include spiritual teachers such as Jesus or Buddha.

You might find that the easiest way to find a wise resource is to simply compile a list of Wise Figures you would like as resources. You can then tap in each of the figures on your list, one at a time. For example, a person might choose Jesus, their grandfather, and Mahatma Gandhi as Wise Figures. They close their eyes, go inside, and bring up the image of Jesus, along with the sense of the wise quality, and begin a short set of bilateral stimulation. If it is getting stronger, bilateral stimulation continues until it feels complete. Then the next figure—their grandfather in his wise aspect—is imagined and tapping resumes. When this feels complete, Gandhi is brought to mind and tapped in. This process repeats with each of the figures they have chosen.

Multiple figures work best for most people. I find that each figure has a different quality that can be called on in different situations. Wisdom called forth by these figures then serves as the resource whenever you need help or advice.

## PRACTICE: TAPPING IN YOUR WISE FIGURES

Begin by compiling a list of Wise Figures; then tap them in, one at a time. The following is a script for tapping in your Wise Figures.

Spend a few moments going inside and quieting your mind.

Think of a figure or figures from your present or past that you associate with wisdom. This can be a person, a spiritual figure, an animal, or even a character from a book or movie. When you imagine the figure, feel the wise quality in your body.

When you have a strong sense of the wise quality of the figure, begin bilateral stimulation. (Use bilateral stimulation for six to twelve right-lefts, then stop and check in with yourself. How was that for you? How do you feel?)

If the wise quality is continuing to strengthen, you can do more bilateral stimulation if you wish. Continue bilateral stimulation as long as you feel the figure and the wise quality strengthening and integrating.

If there is more than one resource, bring the next Wise Figure to mind and tap it in. Repeat this process, tapping in one resource at a time.

## Inner-Wisdom Figures

Another way to develop Wise Figures is to use guided imagery and then invite an Inner-Wisdom Figure to arise in the place being imagined—a process described in four of my previous books and that I will share with you here.

I have found developing and tapping in an Inner-Wisdom Figure to be particularly powerful and helpful, as it arises directly from the unconscious mind. Everyone has within themselves wisdom that they can tap into; discovering a wise voice that originates inside ourselves is inspiring and empowering. Inner-Wisdom Figures can be valuable allies who—once they have been tapped in—can be called on in times of difficulty as sources of support and comfort.

If you have a question or problem or don't know what direction to turn, you can take a moment to go inside yourself, call to mind your Inner-Wisdom Figure, and ask them for guidance while tapping. You can learn to become still and listen for your Inner-Wisdom Figure's advice, then tap more to take in that advice. In this way, these figures can provide guidance and support for you during times of difficulty.

### PRACTICE: TAPPING IN INNER-WISDOM FIGURES

Close your eyes and go inside. Take a deep breath, filling your belly, chest, and throat. Hold the breath a moment, then exhale slowly from your throat, chest, and belly. Relax; let go with the exhalation. Now take another breath. Take your breath in from deep in the earth, filling your belly, chest, and throat. Hold it a few moments. Now exhale, releasing from your throat . . . chest . . . and belly. Relax. Let go. Let yourself settle into the present moment.

When you feel relaxed, imagine going to your Peaceful Place. This is your special place where you are at peace and at ease. Take as much time as you need to find this special place . . . When you are there, notice what you see. Look around. What sounds are you hearing? What are you smelling? What bodily sensations do you notice? How are you feeling in this special place?

As you relax in your Peaceful Place, invite your Inner-Wisdom Figure to join you in this special place. Just allow an image to form that represents your Inner-Wisdom Figure—a wise, kind, loving figure who knows you well. Let it appear in any way that comes, and accept it as it is. It may come in many forms—man, woman, animal, friend, someone you know, or a character from a movie or book.

Accept your Inner-Wisdom Figure as it appears, as long as it seems wise, kind, loving, and compassionate. You will be able to sense its caring for you and its wisdom. Invite it to be comfortable there with you and ask it its name. Accept what comes.

When you have found your Inner-Wisdom Figure, begin to tap. Tap a few times and see how you feel. If it feels good, continue tapping. If it feels bad in any way, stop tapping and return to your Peaceful Place.

You may end here, or you may continue this conversation with your Inner-Wisdom Figure. Tell them about your problem; ask any questions you have concerning this situation, then listen for the answers that come. Listen carefully for the figure's response. You may imagine your figure talking with you, or you may simply have a direct sense of its message in some other way. Allow it to communicate in whatever way seems natural.

If you are uncertain about the meaning of the advice, or if there are other questions you want to ask, continue the conversation until you feel you have learned all you can at this time.

As you consider what your Inner-Wisdom Figure has told you, imagine what your life would be like if you took the advice you have received.

If you have more questions, continue the conversation. When it seems right, thank your Inner-Wisdom Figure for meeting with you and ask it to tell you the easiest, surest method for getting back in touch with it. Realize that you can call another meeting whenever you feel the need for some advice or support. Say goodbye for now, in whatever way seems appropriate, and allow yourself to come back to the room.

## Tapping In the Team

A nice way to provide even more support is to imagine your resources as a team. Think of each resource figure you have tapped in, then imagine all of your resources together. You might imagine them surrounding you, or each may find a specific location in relationship to you. When you can get a good sense of the team, tap them in. Keep tapping as long as it feels good and supportive to you. If it is difficult for you to imagine the different figures together, conjure up the feeling of all your resources and tap that in.

Many people find tapping in the resource team very helpful to them. This team can be called upon when you need support or help in challenging situations. For example, they can be called upon before going to sleep at night or when feeling unsettled or anxious due to something that has occurred at home or work. You can close your eyes, go inside, imagine your resource team, and then tap.

### PRACTICE: TAPPING IN YOUR RESOURCE TEAM

Close your eyes and go inside. Imagine all of your resource figures together as a team. You might imagine them surrounding you, or in any configuration that feels right for you.

When you have a good felt sense of the team, begin to tap. Use bilateral stimulation for six to twelve right-lefts. Then stop and check in with yourself. How was that for you? How do you feel? Tap as long as it feels good and continues to strengthen.

## Summary

### *Finding Support by Calling Up and Tapping In Your Four Foundational Resources*

Now that you have learned how to identify and tap in your Four Foundational Resources, you can use them in a variety of ways. You can use them when you need more support in your life, such as before an event that makes you anxious or when facing a challenge in your personal life. You can call them up before going to sleep at night to help you relax. They can be used whenever you need ease, comfort, courage, power, or wisdom. These resources reside within you and are available whenever you need them. Remember, all you need to do is call them up in your imagination, feel the quality they represent for you, and then add bilateral stimulation. These resources can be included as means to contact inner support as part of many of the practices used in parts three and four of this book. They can also be invoked as part of your regular meditation practice to help settle your mind.

In the next chapter, you will learn about spiritual and natural resources that can be added to your resource tool kit.

# 6

# Spiritual and Natural Resources

Helping to discover, develop, and embody spiritual resources can provide powerful support from within. Spiritual resources, when evoked and tapped in help provide a larger context within which we can view and hold our lives and problems. These resources can help us feel more deeply connected to our spirituality, and they can sustain, empower, and inspire. Spiritual resources can include spiritual figures such as Jesus, Mary, Moses, God, Kwan Yin, the Buddha, angelic beings, spirit guides, or images from nature. Evoking spiritual resources can remind us of our True Nature and essential goodness. After you identify a spiritual figure, you can enhance it with sensory detail to evoke the experience more fully. As you hold in your mind the image and feeling of the figure, add bilateral stimulation to integrate the resource.

If the spiritual figure had appeared in a dream or had been called on in the past for support, memories of these times can be recalled and the positive image and feeling further strengthened with bilateral stimulation. Sometimes spiritual figures will appear in an EMDR session, and that figure can then be evoked and tapped in later for help and support.

My client Molly felt a strong affinity with Kwan Yin, the female Buddha of compassion. Because she had such a deep relationship, we used her as a spiritual resource to support Molly's EMDR work. When Molly brought up the image of Kwan Yin that felt strong and compassionate, we added bilateral stimulation. After a short time of bilateral stimulation, Molly reported that the image strengthened, and she felt a more intimate relationship with Kwan Yin. Afterward, when we did EMDR focusing on memories of childhood abuse, the processing became stuck and an interweave was needed, Molly would call in Kwan Yin to comfort her child self. She could easily imagine Kwan Yin holding and comforting her young self, and she could feel the warmth and safety from a power that felt infinitely compassionate.

Another client contacted a figure she referred to as her childhood "spirit guide." We spent time bringing up memories of help she had gotten from her inner guide. I knew that her spirit guide could be a resource when and if she needed it. It helps to remind ourselves that our spiritual figures are always close at hand; we need only focus inward, recall them, and tap bilaterally to increase our felt connection with them. In this way we can access and tap in our resources when we need the support.

## Angelic Beings, Spirit Guides, Helping Spirits

Over the years many of my clients have reported experiences in their lives or during EMDR sessions of what they call angelic beings, beings of light, spirit guides, or helping spirits. A woman I worked with had an angel spontaneously appear in her processing that was very meaningful to her. This angelic presence then became part of our resource team as we continued to do the work. One woman described such a being sitting at the foot of her bed as a child. This memory returned to her during EMDR processing of a memory from that time. One man recalled such a being and the memory of blocking the being because of a disappointment. As he processed this memory, he sobbed, remembering how he shut out this being. His big aha experience of the session was when he realized the being had never left and was still there. He had blocked the perception of the being, but the being never abandoned him. In many cases when the child told his parents about these meetings, his parents told him it was only his imagination, it didn't exist, and to stop it. The child obeyed the parents, then blocked the connection with the being. Recalling, connecting to, and then tapping in these helping spirits or presences can be powerful resources and provide meaningful support in our lives.

## Higher Power, God, Divine Intelligence, Great Spirit

Higher Power experiences can be recalled and tapped in. This Higher Power might also be called God, the Ground of Being, Pure Consciousness, Divine Intelligence, Mother Nature (Pachamama), or Great Spirit. Contact with a power greater than ourselves provides comfort and a sense that there is something much greater than ourselves directing the unfolding of our lives.

This experience provides wisdom, guidance, and a broader perspective. You may have had an experience of a Higher Power during a time of great stress or during meditation or prayer. You may have touched into your Higher Power during a time of great wonder, such as the birth of a child. Many people experience a sense of something greater than themselves in nature. Learning to listen and attune to the wisdom expressed through the Higher Power can provide a foundation for healing work.

To help connect with your Higher Power, look for memories where you had a sense of something larger than yourself. For some people, nature is a good starting point: the bright, beautiful, powerful sun; a glorious sunset lighting up the sky with brilliant colors; lightning streaking through the dark night; the rising of the full moon. You might feel the power of nature in storms, ocean waves, or the miracle of the unfolding of a flower.

When you contact memories of a Higher Power or a sense of God or Pure Consciousness, you can add bilateral stimulation to strengthen and integrate the feeling more fully. In so doing, you can call on it to provide wisdom and direction to your life.

In one example, a woman I worked with felt disconnected from her spirituality. She wanted to connect again with God, as she defined it. I asked her if she could recall a memory when she had such an experience. She said that she could. I then asked her to close her eyes, go inside, and still her mind. Then I asked her to recall the time when she felt connected to God and to bring back that memory as strongly as she could. Silent, with her eyes closed for a few moments, she nodded her head, signaling me to begin bilateral stimulation. She used small vibrating pulsars under her legs that provided bilateral stimulation. After a few minutes silent with her eyes closed, I could see her state change. Her shoulders dropped and tears appeared at the corners of her eyes. She sighed deeply and then opened her eyes. Wiping tears from her eyes, she reported that with bilateral stimulation she was able to recall the experience of God and feel it in her body. She was obviously moved by what had arisen for her. She said that God was ever present and easily available to her. Details of the memory filled in with bilateral stimulation. All of this occurred very quickly. She left the session smiling and at peace.

### PRACTICE: TAPPING IN A HIGHER POWER

Close your eyes and go inside. Take a few moments to find that quiet place inside yourself. You might take some long, deep breaths to calm your mind. When you are quiet inside, imagine going to your Peaceful Place—your special place where you are at ease and can be fully who you are. Spend as much time as you need in your peaceful sanctuary.

Now, open yourself to experiencing a Higher Power. You may have a direct experience of it in the moment, or you may recall a time when you had a strong feeling of it. Allow yourself to experience it in whatever form it takes. When you have a sense or feeling of a Higher Power, begin to tap. Tap six to twelve times. If you would like to tap longer, you may continue as long as it feels positive and the contact with a Higher Power strengthens.

If you have a particular problem for which you need guidance, or if you have a question or request, you can speak to a Higher Power. Listen for the response. Be open to receiving it in the way in which it comes. You may receive it in words, pictures, or feelings. When you receive the message, begin to tap. Tap as long as it feels positive. Imagine what your life would be like if you followed the guidance of a Higher Power. Tap as you imagine it.

You can contact your Higher Power at any time. It is always with you. You are never separate from it.

## Spiritual Figures

Is there is a spiritual figure you feel an affinity for? Perhaps it is someone from a religious tradition, such as Shiva, Jesus, Ganesha, Mary, Moses, Abraham, Buddha, Vishnu, Kali, the Dalai Lama, or Tara—the female bodhisattva of compassion. It could be a spiritual figure or a spirit guide, helping spirit, angelic being, or ascended ancestor. Is there someone or something you associate with spiritual energy or your spirituality? Such figures can be called upon to support when needed. In times of loneliness or difficulty, or anytime you want a deeper connection to spirituality, these resources can be evoked and tapped in.

Clients have invoked wisdom keepers, power animals, angelic beings, ascended ancestors, spirit guides, or spiritual teachers. It can be helpful to remember that your spiritual figures are always close at hand; you need only focus inward, recall them, and tap to increase your felt connection with them.

### PRACTICE: TAPPING IN SPIRITUAL FIGURES

Close your eyes and go inside. Take some deep, relaxing breaths; let go and release with each exhalation. When you feel more present and relaxed, imagine going to your Peaceful Place, Sacred Place, or Sacred Sanctuary. Tap as you feel yourself there.

Bring to mind someone or something you associate with spirituality. It can be someone you have met, someone you have read about, someone or something from a dream. If you had a spiritual experience that involved the spiritual figure, recall the experience as strongly as you can.

After bringing the figure to mind, focus on visual details. What do they look like? What are they wearing? What expression do they have on their face? If it helps you to feel the spirituality of the figure more, fill in more sensory detail. Notice any sounds, smells, or bodily sensations. Feel the spiritual vibration of the spiritual figure. Sense their spiritual qualities.

As you imagine the figure and feel its spiritual qualities, begin to tap. Tap six to twelve times, right-left, right-left. Tap longer if the resource gets stronger and remains positive. If you would like, you can imagine the qualities of your spiritual figure emanating from it and radiating out to you, where you absorb them into your nervous system. When you can see and feel this, tap. Tap as long as it continues to feel positive. You are taking in the positive qualities of your spiritual resource.

Imagine you're being filled with these qualities. Remember that these are your own inherent qualities that have always resided within you. Whenever you want to connect to the spiritual resource that is associated with the spiritual figure, you can imagine the figure, feel the associated feelings, and tap.

## How I Use My Spiritual Resources

Over the years, I have developed a powerful team of spiritual resources that I connect with every morning as part of my meditation practice. In my twenties I received initiation and empowerment rituals with Lama Yeshe for the deities Green Tara (female Buddha of compassion in action), Vajrapani (Buddha of power and protection), Avalokiteshvara (Buddha of compassion), and Vajrasattva (Buddha of purification). Each morning I visualize these beings and repeat a short version of their mantras. Each one has a specific placement in front of me and to the left or right side. After I do this, I call up my spirit animals. These are animals that have come to me in dreams and visions over the years. Each one has a place. After this, I call in my ascended or spiritual ancestors that don't have forms but feel like light energy coming into my back and above me. If I need more support, I imagine my spiritual teachers and mentors in front of me. I may do this with or without tapping.

After completing this visualization, I begin my meditation of silent, spacious awareness. I will also call in my spiritual resources before teaching or working with a challenging situation. I can also call them in before sleep if I need extra support. I believe doing this practice has helped reinforce the connection to spiritual resources and enabled me to contact them easily during challenging life situations.

## Spiritual Experiences

Many of us have had spiritual experiences that have impacted our lives. These experiences inspire awe and a sense of something much larger than us. If you have had a spiritual experience of some kind during your life, you can recall these and tap them in.

Spiritual experiences—including those had during meditation or prayer, in a dream, in nature, on psychedelic journeys, or during a peak experience—inspire awe, openness, and stillness. Often there is an opening of the heart. Some people can recall spiritual experiences from childhood.

You can strengthen and integrate spiritual experiences by recalling them and adding bilateral stimulation. Recalling and tapping in a spiritual experience may help you more fully integrate the experience into your life. Ask yourself, *How did it affect me? What did I learn from it? How would I like to take the essence of the experience into my life now?* After a response to each of your questions, you can add bilateral stimulation to help integrate the information.

When tapping in the memories of spiritual experiences, you may not reexperience their original power, but evoking the memory and tapping can awaken its feeling or flavor so that it is more available to you. Remembering your deepest experiences can help you feel that your life is spiritually oriented, set within a larger context and meaning than you may have previously believed.

## PRACTICE: TAPPING IN SPIRITUAL EXPERIENCES

You can recall and tap in memories and meanings of these experiences in times when you wish to get in touch with a broader perspective in your life.

Close your eyes and go inside. Bring yourself to the present moment. Feel yourself sitting; make contact with the seat. Take some deep breaths and exhale slowly, letting go and releasing with each breath. Take the time you need to let go and come into the now. You might even tap for a few minutes, right-left, right-left, to calm your mind. If it helps, you can imagine going to your Peaceful Place, Sacred Place, or Sacred Sanctuary first.

Think of a time when you had a spiritual experience: an experience of something larger than yourself that inspired awe. This can be an experience of opening to a higher consciousness, a spiritual insight, an experience of God or a Higher Power, or anything you feel was spiritual. It can include a vision or dream or an experience in nature. You may have experienced it in your adulthood, or it may be a memory from childhood. Invite in whatever comes to you.

Now see if you can recall the experience as much as you can. Where are you? What are you doing? If it applies to this experience, bring in sensory information. What are you seeing, hearing, smelling, feeling in your body? Notice how you feel inside. Now open to the experience. Allow it to unfold in you. Take in the information it offers you. Let it fill you with its flavor—the essence of its message. When you have a feeling for the experience, begin to tap. Tap six to twelve times, right-left, right-left. If it continues to strengthen and integrate, continue tapping until it feels complete to you.

Sit for some moments with the feeling. You can recall this experience and tap to contact and strengthen it whenever you feel the need. You can also imagine ways to integrate/incorporate these experiences into your day-to-day life. For example, if you had an experience of great love with your heart opened wide, you can recall where you were when you had this experience and the expansion in your heart and then add bilateral stimulation. The message you received was that love was everywhere and that it was abundant and limitless. Tap bilaterally as you imagine taking this feeling and message into your life.

## Spiritual Teachings

When I go on retreat, I take with me books by spiritual teachers that inspire me. Reading their words and then sitting with them in silence allows the meaning behind the words to resonate. It is an apperception of the meaning that strikes deeply, a remembering of my True Self—a homecoming.

Along with insights and life lessons, you can recall and tap in spiritual teachings that are significant to you. You may have been moved by teachings from a spiritual tradition that resonates with you, or touched by a spiritual teaching. Despite these experiences, many of us find that we struggle to apply these teachings in our lives.

You may have been moved by something you have read in spiritual literature or poetry, or that you heard from wise teachers or elders. Think about the most important spiritual teachings you have read or received, or the spiritual teachings you wish to live by more fully. You can also think of a particular teaching, meditate on it a while, then add bilateral stimulation to integrate it more fully. Try to imagine what your life would be like if you lived with the wisdom of this teaching, and then add bilateral stimulation. In this way, you can integrate this wisdom and make it your own and use it to better orient yourself in your life. Take time to contemplate teachings that are important to you on a regular basis, then tap them in.

PRACTICE: TAPPING IN SPIRITUAL TEACHINGS

Close your eyes, go inside, and spend a few moments calming your mind. Review in your mind the most important teachings you have read or received. You might want to focus on just one teaching or saying for the day. What specific teaching would you like to focus on today? As you contemplate the teaching and can feel the wisdom in it, tap. Tap as long as it feels positive.

Bring up any additional teachings you would like to tap in and take some time to add bilateral stimulation to each one.

You can finish up by imagining taking the teaching into your life. What would your life look like if you lived with this teaching? When you have a strong sense of this, tap it in, continuing to tap for as long as it feels positive.

## Nature as a Resource

Nature can inspire a sense of deep peace and be a generous source of positive resource images. Nature can connect us with something larger than ourselves and help to anchor us in the here and now. Remembering this connection returns us to something so vital and nourishing, and we can do this in a number of ways, including through memories of nature experiences, nature forms and sacred places, walking or meditating in nature, and composting problematic emotions or energies. Even if you live in a city, it can be helpful to locate land features—hills, plateaus, plains, valleys, deserts—near where you live.

### Memories of Nature Experiences

You can recall any memories or experiences in nature that brought you a feeling of well-being. It could be hiking in the mountains, fishing by a river, snorkeling with manta rays in Hawaii, swimming with dolphins, or planting flowers in a garden. Think about your favorite places from nature that bring a sense of peace. These can be places you've been to or places that you create in your imagination. The imagery and feeling states that these places evoke can be tapped in with bilateral stimulation.

## Nature Forms and Sacred Places

Near my home, there's a path along a lovely little creek with beautiful trees. Mount Tamalpais is the major land feature nearby. If we bring to mind the major land features like this near where we live and tap them in, the images can help us connect more fully to the land and provide grounding. In addition, nature forms and places can be used as resources even if you have never been to the place or seen it. There are some landforms that are sacred and very powerful, such as Mount Kailash in the Himalayas, Mount Shasta in California, and Kilauea in Hawaii. The vast sea can create a feeling of openness when imagined. There are enormous ancient trees that carry a sacred quality, such as the giant sequoias, the Major Oak in England, the bodhi tree in India, and the kapok tree in the Amazon. Places such as the Grand Canyon, Chaco Canyon, Monument Valley, and other places carry a sacred quality and when imagined evoke a power of the place.

Is there any place or nature form that is significant to you? For example, for many years I have had dreams of a majestic snow-covered mountain that inspires a sense of great awe and feels connected to Consciousness itself. It is shaped like a diamond and has a numinous quality. When I asked inside myself for the name, Mount Meru came. Mount Meru, or Kailash as it is also called, is a sacred mountain for Hindus, Jains, and Tibetan Buddhists. When I call to mind this mountain and feel the energy of it, it evokes a sacred feeling; a connection to the earth, timeless consciousness, clarity of mind, and the vastness of now.

## Walk or Meditate in Nature

Walking in a natural setting can also be resourcing. After my son was killed, I found that walking every day on the wooded path by the creek near our home helped me live through what felt unlivable. I could see the old craggy trees with deep roots that clung to the creek banks, hear the birdsong and chirps of frolicking squirrels, and feel the earth solidly beneath my feet as I put one foot in front of the other. The immersion in nature filled my senses, and walking provided bilateral stimulation.

Meditating in a natural setting can also be resourcing. Near our home is a trail that leads along a creek to a small waterfall that cascades into two small pools of water. Above the pools are two large rocks where my husband and I sit silently to meditate, taking in the sound of the tinkling creek, birdsong, and the wind in the trees. It feels like a sacred place, a place where people have visited for thousands of years for silent communion with nature and themselves. When I sit on the rock, I open to nature sounds, listening, and then my mind quiets as I drop into the silent nowness. This sitting practice is nourishing to body and soul, and afterward I feel refreshed and renewed.

When sitting in nature, see if you can find a place where you will not be disturbed. Then sit silently and just listen. Open to the sounds without forcing it. Let the sounds come to you rather than you going to the sounds. Try not to interpret or even identify what you are hearing. Let the sounds just be sounds. If there are sensations you notice, such as the breeze on your cheek, just notice that. Open to the scents of the place, such as the scent of the trees, flowers, or water. Invite your body to relax and just be. If you feel it will be helpful, as you immerse yourself in the place, add bilateral stimulation, such as tapping on the sides of your legs. You can also later recall this place of peace and use it as a resource for replenishment.

## Composting Problematic Emotions or Energies

Another thing that can be done with nature resources is to compost emotions or energies that you do not wish to carry. You can ask to send these undesired energies into the earth where it travels down through the roots of trees. For example, if you are holding distressing feelings or energies you have picked up that you wish to release, you can imagine a tree with deep roots and offer these things to the tree as compost that nourishes it. In this way you can feel it begin to release from your system.

When I was deep in grief after the death of my son, walking every day by the creek near our home allowed me to connect to the trees with deep roots and the branches that grew in twisted, crooked ways as they reached for the light. I imagined giving my unbearable grief to the mother tree, as I called her, an ancient one who had lived through storms, droughts, and windstorms with deep roots that could carry my grief to the earth as nourishment for new life. It helped to see wildflowers blooming and the little creek flowing, tadpoles swimming in small pools, tiny froglets hidden among the leaves. All of this was a reminder of life continuing. You can tap in connections to nature and the natural world for grounding, comforting, and healing.

### PRACTICE: TAPPING IN NATURE

Close your eyes and go inside. Take a few moments to settle yourself and quiet your mind. Now think of a place in nature that you feel a connection to. It is a place where you feel at peace, your mind silent and at ease. It could be a place you have been to before or that has appeared in a dream or vision. It could be a sacred or spiritual place or a place where you feel a connection to the natural world.

Let an image or memory appear and accept what comes as long as it is entirely positive.

Notice what you see in this place. Look around. What do you hear? Are there any scents? What sensations do you feel, such as the breeze on your skin or the warmth of the sun on your face? What do you notice in your body? How do you feel in this place?

When you can sense this nature place and feel what it evokes for you, begin to tap, right-left, right-left. Continue to tap as long as it feels good to you and the feelings strengthen. Stop if anything unpleasant arises and return to the nature image. You may find another nature place if the one you have chosen has negative feelings arising.

Is there a word or phrase that represents this place for you? Take note of it.

Whenever you wish to recall this nature place to remind you of its gifts, you can bring it to mind or use the words you have for it and tap bilaterally.

## Big Love

Evoking spiritual resources can be a powerful part of our practice, and Big Love is another spiritual resource that we can access and tap in. Big Love is foundational to Multidimensional Integrative Healing and is a love that is vast and boundaryless. When it's experienced, it fills us with blissful light that expands our hearts and extends outward, radiating like a brilliant sun dissolving separateness between all living things so that there is an experience of unity. Some might to refer this as Divine Love. This love is universal and nonpersonal. When experienced, it is recognized as something that has always been there in the background of awareness.

I have been fortunate to have experienced this several times in my life and recognized that it was this Big Love that is inseparable from the consciousness that is the background of all life.

I mentioned earlier that my teacher Lama Thubten Yeshe emanated Big Love, and it was the energetic signature experience experience of being in his presence. When he would enter the meditation hall, bowing to all assembled, smiling broadly, a full body rush of love energy would wash over me and the room would fill with this Big Love energy. This energy is beyond compassion or loving-kindness, though they are contained within it. It is universal energy and exists always. Whenever I have been in the presence of His Holiness the Dalai Lama, hearing him speak, receiving teaching or initiations, I have experienced this vast Big Love as well.

I have also experienced the energy of Big Love when doing EMDR, especially when assisting clients in connecting to spiritual resources. For many people, when they connect with what they describe as "God's Love," or Jesus or Kwan Yin as loving, nurturing figures, this Big Love energy will fill the two of us and the room we are in. Some clients who have had near-death experiences or communication with loved ones who have crossed over will describe the immensity of this Big Love. One woman's mother, who had died several years before, spoke to her after an EMDR session and said, "If you only knew how much love there is, you would never be afraid."

In another instance, a woman volunteered to do a demonstration of Attachment-Focused EMDR in front of an audience with me. She told me that she had not been loved as a child and continued to suffer from an inner emptiness and a sense of not belonging or deserving love. When we tried to find Nurturing Figures, she told me there were none she could think of. She could not recall being loved or cared for ever in her life. I told her she did not have to remember being loved, just a figure who represented that for her. Still, she could not think of anyone or anything that she could connect with in a meaningful way.

She was beginning to feel as though she couldn't do the resourcing when I asked her if she had given love to anyone or anything else or had any experience of that, even a spiritual experience. She told me that she once had a spiritual experience of God as a loving presence. I thought, *Wonderful, now we have something.* I asked her to close her eyes and recall that experience as strongly as she could. With her eyes closed, she nodded her head, asserting that she had been able to recall it. I then instructed her to stay connected with that experience of God as a loving presence as I tapped her knees right-left, right-left in a gentle, slow rhythm. After only a few moments of tapping I felt a rush of golden light pour down through the top of my head, filling my entire body with light that felt like Divine Love. I continued to tap as she reported the same experience I was having. Tears streamed down both our faces. It was like we were plugged into a circuit of Divine Love light that filled us.

I continued to tap and feel this stream of golden light pour through me for several minutes until my client nodded her head that it was time to stop. She opened her eyes and met my gaze, both of us deeply moved by what we had just experienced. Then when we looked around at the audience, I could see that they too had been filled with this love light. Many in the room had tears in their eyes. We all sat in silence for some minutes in awe.

After this, we had a break, and the audience slowly left the room for lunch. During this time, another woman came up to the client and asked her if she could give her a hug. She said she felt compelled to do this and asked her if it would it be okay with her. The client agreed, and the woman embraced her in her arms. As I watched this, I was moved. There was so much love there. After the embrace, they gazed into each other's eyes, spoke a little, and then parted.

We reconvened after lunch, and the client and I resumed, establishing her resource figures. When I asked her about Nurturing Figures, she immediately named the woman who had hugged her. She said the Divine Love that she had experienced had taken form as the woman who embraced her. During our EMDR session, she was able to call in the image of that woman to help heal the hurt she experienced as an unloved child.

It is this Big Love that is an essential foundation for our Multidimensional Integrative Healing work. When the healing we do is held in Big Love, even the intention of holding it this way sets the feeling and safety of the work. Big Love is holding both the therapist and client in the space of healing.

### PRACTICE: TAPPING IN BIG LOVE

Close your eyes and go inside. Take a few moments to settle yourself and calm your mind.

Think of a time in your life when you have experienced Big Love. This is a love that is vast, purely radiant, unconditional, and boundless. You might call it Divine Love or God's love. You may recall a time from your childhood when you felt deeply loved, a time when you felt great love for another, or a spiritual or religious experience of Divine Love, God's love, or however you describe it for yourself. If you can recall just a little of this experience, that is okay. When you have a sense of that love feeling, begin to tap. Tap right-left, right-left, allowing the feeling to grow. You might feel it in your heart and invite that feeling to expand. Continue to tap as long as it feels good to you.

## Summary

### *Embodying and Utilizing Spiritual and Natural Resources Through Resource Tapping*

You have now been introduced to many ways to connect with and tap in your spiritual and natural resources. Tapping in spiritual teachers, teachings, and experiences helps us to more fully embody and utilize these resources so that we can bring them more fully into our lives. Our spiritual resources can be integrated into our daily meditation practice, which helps to reinforce the connection to them and enables us to contact them easily during challenging life situations.

Nature resources help to bring comfort, grounding, and support, connecting us to that which sustains us all. All of these resources can be used as needed, especially during times of great stress and unease.

In the next chapter you will learn about ancestral resources that can be drawn upon to help support us in our lives. You'll also learn ways to bring healing to our ancestral lineages when there has been trauma and/or unwholesome patterns and messages.

# 7

# Ancestral Resources

We can draw from ancestral resources to bring help and healing to ourselves in the present. We can also bring resources to the ancestral lineage to help heal the lineage. An ancestor is one from whom a person is descended and who is usually more remote in the line of descent than a grandparent. Our ancestry can include recent or remembered ancestors: deceased parents, grandparents, children, siblings, and other kin who knew us during our lives. Ancestry can also include earlier generations who are remembered through stories told in families or discovered through genealogical research.

I would also expand the definition of ancestry beyond genetics to include spiritual ancestry. Spiritual ancestry is a felt connection to a people and place that is not from our genetic lineage. This may or may not be a lineage associated with past lives. For example, I have always felt a strong affinity with Tibet and Tibetans. As soon as I met my spiritual teacher, Lama Thubten Yeshe, in 1975, I felt a homecoming, a remembering, a comfort and ease with the rituals and practices that I was introduced to that could not be explained by my history or background. When I am with Tibetans, I feel like they are my people. Several psychics have told me over the years that I am from the East, and one placed me in Tibet. I have a strong felt sense of lineage connection to these people, practices, and places. I have had many dreams, visions, and journeys that have taken me to places in Tibet that have felt significant and deeply spiritual.

I have felt as well a connection to the Celtic people of northern England and Ireland who I believe are from my genetic/familial lineage. As soon as I was introduced to the ancient practices and the land on a trip I took to England, Scotland, Wales, and Ireland in 1977, I felt a homecoming and recognition. It was in the ancient places of standing stones, stone circles, and wells—along with the land itself—that I felt this feeling of home. I did not feel this in the churches or places associated with Christianity or more modern times. My connection to this area goes back to pre-Christian times, when the people practiced rituals associated with nature and the spirit world, practices that were forbidden under the Romans and Christian conquerors.

## Healing Through the Great Expanse of Ancestral Resources

According to the psychotherapist and ritualist Daniel Foor in his book *Ancestral Medicine*, along all lineages there is a threshold beyond which names, faces, and family stories are forgotten.[1] The dead whose names are no longer remembered include the majority of our ancestors, going back thousands of years. When I open my awareness to this larger view, I feel an expansion of consciousness and a recognition that I have been viewing life through a narrow lens, one that records time from the advent of Christianity. I realized, too, that the Gregorian calendar counts time beginning with the birth of Christ, as if time or human beings did not exist before then. When I expand into time before then, following the sense of my ancestral line back thousands of years before the Roman invasion and the Christian conquest, I connect to a feeling of life that was nature-based, spiritual, and harmonious.

Most of us in the United States, except for the Native peoples, have come from other lands. For African Americans, expanding into the time before their ancestors were brought to the Americas as slaves—a time when they were connected to traditions, family, spiritual practices, and land—can provide a broader perspective and context. If our lens is expanded beyond the period of enslavement to times of peaceful living in a culture that includes connection to the earth and one's people, it changes our view and can change how we feel about ourselves. Even though all peoples have in their histories times of war, conflict, and scarcity, there also exist times of peace and abundance. For the Native peoples of the Americas—whose ancestors were murdered; their land taken by European invaders; and their children kidnapped and forced to live in residential schools that stripped them of their language, culture, spiritual practices, and family connections while indoctrinating them into Christianity—these traumas have had profound intergenerational impact. But when the lens is expanded to before the time of the invaders, to a time when they lived in harmony with the earth and plants, the animals, and their spiritual traditions, it changes the perspective and can bring a felt sense of well-being. Time begins to expand in multiple dimensions, and we are part of a greater web of life, an ancestry that is long and complex and can help hold us.

This chapter provides ways to find resilient, wholesome resources in our lineages that can be used for healing and to support us in our lives. These can include healthy, whole, wise ancestral lineage; an ancestral helping spirit—that is, a healthy, whole ancestor who can be a wise resource or guide; known ancestors; resources from the ancestral land; and the ancestral well or spring.

When some of us begin to explore our ancestry and lineages, we may become overwhelmed by the enormity of trauma. Yet if we go back far enough within our ancestral lineages, there exists a wealth of resources and resilience. It is like we are casting our net wider than from our known ancestry and exploring time before anyone in our family has information or memories. There also exists in everyone's lineage healthy, whole ancestry that may be unremembered but can be accessed and used as resources for healing work. These resources can derive from our genetic or spiritual lineages. Using guided imagery techniques, we can discover resources in our lineages such as abundance, love, peace, well-being, courage, and power that can help us in our lives.

## Healthy, Whole Ancestral Lineage

We all have healthy and unhealthy ancestry in our lineages, times of scarcity and times of plenty, people who were abusive and hurtful, and those who were wise and compassionate. When we allow ourselves to go far back in our ancestral lineages, we can find wholesome resources that can help us in the present.

One way to discover and draw healing from wholesome ancestral resources is to journey back to a time when there was peace, harmony, and wisdom in the ancestral lineage. When we go back further than remembered times, past what our family has recounted and remembered, we can discover ancestral resources that can help us in the present. This is time hundreds, maybe thousands of years ago and is not associated in any way with traumas. You don't have to be limited by anything you have been told or you have learned. With this technique we are not looking for a memory or anything that requires authentication. What we want to discover is a sense of a time and place, a felt sense, a knowing that has a reality of its own. When we locate a scene, which may or may not include other sensory information—smells, sounds, and body experiences—it resonates with a place inside us that recognizes it. This scene could connect to a genetic or a spiritual lineage/ancestry. What is important, too, is that scenes that arise with a feeling state resonate as significant, and the information that they hold can be integrated and tapped in with bilateral stimulation. As a result, it changes how we feel and perceive ourselves and our world. The information that we connect with in this exercise can also be used to heal the ancestral lineage.

## PRACTICE: FINDING HEALTHY, WHOLE ANCESTRAL TIME

When you try this practice, put your thinking mind aside and let your mind take you back in time to a time of plenty, wholesomeness, and well-being. It is important to accept what comes. It might take you a few minutes to land somewhere that feels significant. You might use bilateral stimulation in whatever form appeals to you, including rattling or drumming, to facilitate this process. Discover what works best for you. When you feel you have arrived at a time and place, don't interpret or try to figure out what has come up. Instead, just explore where you have arrived and take in its meaning. You cannot know if what has come to you is "real." This is not important. What we are looking for is a healthy, whole, wise, energetic feeling state associated with imagery or a sense of a place and time. Upon arriving there, notice how it feels. Where do you feel it in your body? If you did not use bilateral stimulation in your journey, you might want to add it after discovering the resource. This can serve to help integrate more fully the feeling state and the message from that time.

Close your eyes and go inside. Take three deep breaths and slowly let them go, dropping into the now. You might take a moment to go to your Peaceful Place. See if you can set your thinking mind aside. (If you wish, you can begin bilateral stimulation in whatever form appeals to you, including drumming or rattling, and keep it going throughout this process.)

Now ask to go back to a time in your ancestral lineage when there was peace and well-being. Ask for a time when there was enough, and there was peace and harmony in the community. Find a time when your ancestors were well, balanced, and guided by wisdom. Let whatever comes up come up without censoring it. Go back hundreds, maybe thousands of years. See what appears for you.

When something arises, notice what you see. Look around. Open your senses and explore this place. Notice what you hear. Who is there with you? Spend some time there learning what you need to know from your lineage, from your ancestors. (If you haven't begun bilateral stimulation, you can begin here after you have discovered the healthy ancestral time.) If you have found a time and if it feels right to you, you can begin to tap. Tap right-left, right-left, as long as it feels positive and helpful. Stop right away if it does not.

Spend as much time as you would like soaking in the feeling of your healthy, wise, whole ancestral time. When you feel like you have what you need for now, ask that this new knowledge, this energetic knowing, be carried up through your ancestral line. It can be like bringing this newfound energy up through an energetic channel or cord from the past into the present. Also, if it feels right to you, you might see if this healthy, wise ancestral energy/resource has a color or temperature of some kind. If it does, ask that this be brought forward. Keep bringing this resourceful ancestral energy forward in time until you feel it in your present life, in your present circumstance.

Are there words that briefly capture this wholesome ancestry? Is there a symbol or something to help you to recall it? Again, if you want, you can add bilateral stimulation.

If you wish, you can invite this ancestral wisdom energy into your future and the future lineage. Tap if this feels right to you.

If it feels right for you, you can ask that this ancestral resource energy be brought to ancestral traumas to be healed. Spend time bringing this ancestral healing energy there. If it feels right for you, you might tap, right-left, right-left, as you imagine bringing this resource to these places. If it doesn't feel right to you at this time, you might do it later if you wish, adding this in after connecting with the healthy, whole ancestral energy

In my experience with this exercise of traveling back to healthy, whole ancestral time, what came to me was a grassy area with oak trees, a stream, and people. There was enough food and what was needed for a good life. I could sense that there was ease of being and peace. It was safe. I asked what words I could bring back to describe this. The words *peace*, *safety*, and *enough*—enough food, and "I am enough, I have enough"—immediately came to mind. When I imagined bringing this feeling up the present time, it felt good. I felt resourced by it.

## Connecting with Ancestral Resilience

Sometimes we feel there is something in our family system or ancestry that keeps us from what we need to live fully. There may be old patterns or beliefs that hold us back. There may be a feeling of lack that keeps us stuck. You can travel back in time to find resilience or other resources in your ancestry.

A Singaporean colleague of mine found the ancestral resourcing to be a great source of support, especially with her Asian clients, for whom cultural aspects of deep spirituality, filiality, and family ties play an important role. She reported that it was easier for these clients to lean into their ancestors' lineage without any resistance. Based on her clinical observations, she also found this work to have tremendous potential in building resources, increasing the nervous system's capacity, widening the window of tolerance, as well as increasing safety and stabilizing clients. The following is her description of using the ancestral resilience work with a client.

> Aisha, a fifty-year-old Malaysian woman, was seeing me for anxiety and relationship problems. She had done trauma work with me using EMDR. During one of her weekly sessions, she reported feeling stuck. She was running low on funds and complained of a feeling of scarcity. This felt like an old, entrenched feeling with life-limiting beliefs. I sensed that she was carrying something from her ancestry that was blocking her in the present. I thought it would be a good idea to tap into abundance in her ancestors' lineage and bring it to her present.
>
> I invited her to go back in time in her ancestral lineage to a time when there was abundance. To my surprise, she straightaway went to her spiritual lineage. She reported that she saw Ibrahim giving her true fruits—one for herself and one to be shared with the community. After she discovered this, I helped her expand it by asking her to notice detailed sensory information, and then I added bilateral stimulation. After doing this, I observed an instant shift in the client's physiology. Her posture became more open, her face relaxed, and her breathing deepened.
>
> She told me she saw herself wearing a golden armor that was light but strong. She could remove it whenever she liked and with whomever she wanted. Further, in processing this newfound abundance and protection, she realized whatever was bothering her were small miniatures shooting her. She said that she was able to dodge those arrows even though she was

confused about why they were shooting at her. She said she felt strong enough to move past those.

Later, during debriefing, she mentioned that she had abundance from her ancestors that is available to her. She also said that she felt strong enough to tackle the situations in her life. These positive beliefs were enhanced with bilateral stimulation, helping to integrate them more fully.

## PRACTICE: BRIDGING TO ANCESTRAL RESILIENCE

For this exercise, we are going to go back to find a time in our ancestral lineage when there was resilience, a time when we were able to overcome difficulties.

Close your eyes and go inside. Take some breaths, find your calm center. Put your thinking mind aside. Take some time and imagine going to your Peaceful Place.

Ask to go back to a time of resilience in your ancestry. Go back as far as you can without censoring it. It can be from a long, long time ago—even thousands of years. Let whatever arises arise without judgment. We are looking for the seeds of resilience. Notice what comes.

When you have landed somewhere, take in the scene. What do you see, feel, hear, smell? Can you sense the resilience in your lineage? When you have a good felt sense of this, you can add bilateral stimulation.

Now, if this feels right to you, bring this feeling up your ancestral lineage to the present time. Feel it in your body and your energetic system. Take all the time you need. If you wish, you can add bilateral stimulation to increase the feeling.

If you wish, you can bring this sense of resilience into the future. Bring this up your ancestral line into future generations.

## Recalling Known Ancestors

You can recall and tap in remembered family members or ancestors. Are there people in your lineage known to you that you want to connect with to receive the helpful guidance they can provide? You can think of them or imagine them, and then you can add bilateral simulation to tap them in.

You can also use guided imagery or journeying to find a wise, emotionally healthy, well-balanced ancestor. When the wise ancestor is found, you can use bilateral simulation to tap them in. After doing this, you can call on them whenever you need help or support. When I did this work, I discovered a strong spiritual resource, an ancestor who was like a spirit guide. She was wise and powerful. I felt her behind me with a very large presence. I believe she was one of my ancestral guides.

### PRACTICE: FINDING A WISE ANCESTOR/GUIDE

Close your eyes and go inside. Take three deep breaths, then slowly let them go, dropping into the now. You might take a moment to go to your Peaceful Place. See if you can set your thinking mind aside. Ask to go back to a time in your ancestral lineage when there was peace and well-being; a time when there was enough, and there was peace and harmony in the community. Ask for a time when your ancestors were well, balanced, and guided by wisdom. Let in whatever comes up without censoring it. Go back hundreds, maybe thousands of years. See what appears. When something arises, notice what you see. Notice what you hear. Open your senses and explore this place. Now ask for someone from that time who lived a good life. This person is wise, compassionate, and emotionally balanced. Take a moment and allow this person to come to mind. Stay open to what comes. What do they look like? What does it feel like to be in their presence? Does this person have a name? Spend some time there learning what you need to know from this ancestor. Would this ancestor be willing to be an ancestral guide?

If yes, ask if it is alright to create an energetic connection or cord between the two of you that can allow a transfer of their wisdom and healing energy into you and your lineage. Notice where this cord connects to your body. This is a conduit to ancestral-wisdom energy that can resource and support you and your loved ones. As you feel the energetic connection to the wisdom of this ancestral figure, you can tap if you wish to strengthen and integrate it. Allow yourself to open the energetic channel from the then to the now with information that is helpful and resourcing for you. Notice where you feel this in your body. If you have found a wise ancestor, and if it feels right to you, you can begin to tap. Tap right-left, right-left, for as long as it feels positive and helpful. Stop right away if it does not. Spend as much time as you would like soaking in the feeling of your healthy, wise, whole ancestor.

When you feel like you have what you need for now, imagine bringing this new knowledge, this energetic knowing from your ancestor up through your ancestral line. It can be like bringing this newfound energy up through an energetic channel or cord from the past into the present. Keep bringing it forward until you feel it in your present life, in your present circumstance. Know that you can connect with the energetic feeling or signature of this ancestor by calling their name or remembering the place you found them. This is your ancestral-wisdom figure that you can call on as a resource to support you in your life and healing work.

If you wish, you can invite the wisdom energy from this ancestor into your future and the future lineage. Tap if this feels right to you.

(What follows might be done in a separate session. Add this in after connecting with the healthy, whole ancestral energy.) If it feels right for you, you might invite this ancestral resource energy to help heal ancestral traumas that you identify. Spend time bringing this ancestral healing energy there. If it feels right for you, you might tap, right-left, right-left, as you imagine bringing this resource to these places.

## Tapping In Cultural and Ancestral Traditions

You can also connect to cultural and ancestral traditions. These traditions can come from your genetic or spiritual lineage. Even though many of these traditions may be lost, you might be able to find remnants of them that can connect you to your lineage. You can inquire, *What cultural or ancestral traditions do I want to connect to? What are the healing traditions, songs, dances, chants?* Look for ways to reclaim the traditions. You might name and list them and then tap them in. Discover the language or words that were used in ceremony. Many of these ancient languages have been lost, but there are still some words or phrases that can be found. What sacred objects connect to the lineage? When these things are activated and felt, you can use bilateral simulation to enhance and help integrate them. Perhaps you recall stories of dancing and drumming in a circle with chanting. As you recall and can feel the energy of these traditions, add bilateral stimulation. What are the things that are in your tradition, in your lineage, that you know are meaningful? Recall them, and then tap them in.

## Connecting to and Resourcing from the Ancestral Land

During times of great stress and upheaval, I have found it helpful to recall and tap in ancestral land. This is land that we feel a deep connection to that may be a place we have been to or a place we have heard or read about associated with our people that resonates deeply with us. This is a place that feels meaningful to us. It could be from our genetic or spiritual ancestry. Recalling and resonating with this land can ground us, helping to bring us into the present moment when we feel fearful and ungrounded. Connecting to the land can bring a feeling of belonging, comfort, and peace. This resource can help especially during times when you feel lost and rootless. You may know the place already or you may use the guided practice to find such a place.

### PRACTICE: RESOURCING FROM THE ANCESTRAL LAND

Take a few moments to go inside and quiet your mind. You might imagine putting your thinking mind aside.

Ask to go back in time to find your ancestral land. Go back as far as you can. It might be a place you know well or that appears to you spontaneously. Let an image arise. Don't censor it.

What does it feel like being there? How do you feel when you connect to it? Is there a particular place on the land that feels significant to you?

When you have a good sense of this land and place, along with the feeling you have embodied, begin to tap. Tap as long as it feels good to you.

If it feels right for you, you can invite the feeling of this connection to the land into your life now. This is a resource you can draw upon for strength and support. Is there something that symbolizes this place? A word or phrase to describe it? You can use these words, anytime you wish, to help you recall the connection to the land when you wish to draw from the support it brings to you.

## Visting the Ancestral Well or Spring

According to Jean Schneider, one way to connect with the best in our ancestry is to visit the ancestral well. In premodern times, a well, a spring, or even a river was the source of water for our ancestors. It was the most important place, a place that was honored with ritual blessings and ceremony at times throughout the year. Water means life. Without water, there is no life for us, for the animals, for the plants, for the land.

Doing an ancestral well visit will appear differently for everyone. For some, it is a fountain in a place or room. For others, it is a place in nature—a spring or well in the earth. It may be a creek or river. It may be a real physical place or a nonphysical place that represents the best of your ancestry.

The first time I was guided to my ancestral well was a time I was feeling very low and emotionally exhausted. Here is what I wrote afterward:

> I was guided to find my ancestral well, the place of wisdom from my ancestors. I was directed to find the door. What came to me spontaneously in imagery was a huge granite boulder with a door that opened into a cave. It was a large cave, and it didn't make me feel trapped. I entered using a light and discovered it was a crystal cave with a mirrorlike pool. I crossed the pool and sat cross-legged on the other side. It was a pool for visions. It was a sacred, secret, ancestral crystal cave. I lighted sconces on the sides of the cave that reflected light on the

crystals. It was full of reflected light. I entered the very cold, clear water of the pool and submerged myself. Afterward I felt refreshed. Though I recognized it as a cave for me to go for visions and wisdom, I didn't receive any information and didn't see any visions reflected in the pool.

The experience felt significant. I felt renewed afterward and connected to something very old. I sensed that it was someplace in England. It had taken me out of this time and into a timeless continuity. I was connected to a greater, older lineage of seers, healers, wise women. I felt less grief and more awe. This was astonishing, as it was not at all what I was expecting. I would never have thought to enter a cave to find the ancestral well. The cave reminded me of the crystal geode I brought home from a trip to Madagascar, which I have now placed on my desk as an anchor and reminder of this sacred ancestral place of wisdom, of renewal and resilience. This experience felt connected to my genetic/biological ancestry.

The second time I did this it brought me to my spiritual ancestry. I was leading a group at Esalen to find their sacred well or spring. During the practice, I saw a dirt path on a vast green expanse, like a plain. The spring was there. I was surprised—there were no trees, rocks, or shade. The pool was like a mirror. I could see the moon and the bright stars reflected there. Animals came to drink. It was a spring for prophesy. It was for healing. I was a healer, a wise woman. I looked into the pool, and there was light coming from the bottom. It was silver light. I was drawn to follow the light down. It was bottomless. I realized it was a portal into another world or dimension. I felt the sacredness of this spring. I was surprised that I was alone. No other people or trees. I didn't recognize this as somewhere I had been in other journeys. Then I realized I was not in England but in Tibet. I was up high on the Tibetan Plateau. I believed there were immense mountains nearby. I could feel that as I wrote this. There was a feeling of expansive space. Big sky, vast plains, and immense mountains. But the spring was in the middle of this plain. It wasn't obvious, but there it was. This was my ancestral spring. The spring of seeing, prophesy, healing, and wisdom.

### PRACTICE: JOURNEYING TO THE ANCESTRAL WELL OR SPRING

When we journey to and connect with the ancestral well or spring, we access a source of healing and healing energy. Later we can recall that place and use it as a resource to imbue us with the sense of that place and its sacred energy, bringing the then into the now. As with the other resources, you can use bilateral stimulation to help enhance and integrate the experience if you wish.

Close your eyes and go inside. Take a few moments to quiet your mind. Feel yourself sitting, take some deep breaths, and release into the present moment. Put your thinking mind aside.

You are going on a journey to visit your ancestral well or spring. This is a sacred place from your ancestry that holds the best of your ancestry. When you journey to your ancestral well, you can receive gifts from your ancestors. It can be helpful to set your intentions before you go: What is the purpose of your journey? What are you seeking to find? Is this a time in your life when you are seeking wisdom? Do you wish to find strength? Are there messages from your ancestors that you hope to receive? The ancestral well or spring holds the best of your ancestry, the vitality and special talents of your lineage that are passed down within your lineages. By coming to the ancestral well, you can receive this from your ancestry. As you journey to your ancestral well, if it feels right for you, you can begin any kind of bilateral stimulation. You can rattle, drum, tap the sides of your legs, use Eagle Wings Flapping, or tap either shoulder.

Now ask to travel back in time to discover your ancestral well or spring. Go back as far as you can. Drop back further and further. Take the time that you need. You might discover a door that opens to this place. Open the door and enter the place where you will discover your ancestral well. Invite a pathway to your ancestral well to appear. Your ancestral well may appear as an image or a sense of a place.

Once the place arrives, introduce yourself; say your name. What do you see in this place? Look around. How are you being invited to interact with the ancestral well or spring? Are you being invited to drink the water or splash the water on yourself? Is there anyone at the well? If it is a spring or a river, do you wish to bathe in the water? If there is a wise ancestor or guardian there, spend time with this person. Ask any questions you might have and listen to their response. Do they have a message for you or words of wisdom?

Rest here at the ancestral well or spring and feel into the energy of this place. Allow yourself to attune to the energetic signature of the beauty and vitality of your ancestry. What are you receiving from this place? What are the gifts?

Sometimes in order to accept the gifts of the ancestral well or spring, you must be in a state of receiving and readiness. What are you receiving this time? Take note of it. Every time you go to this place, you may receive even more, because you have room for it or are ready to receive more. The gifts at the ancestral well and spring are endless. Spend as much time as you wish at this sacred place taking in the gifts of your ancestry.

When you feel that you have received all that is possible at this visit, stop bilateral stimulation and open your eyes. Take time to write down what you experienced. You might even visually represent it by drawing.

Know that you can revisit your ancestral well whenever you feel called to reconnect with the wisdom it provides you. When you reattune to the strength of your ancestry regularly, you can embody more of it.

## Summary

### *Drawing Inspiration and Resilience from Your Ancestry*

You have now been introduced to many ways you can connect with and draw inspiration and resilience from your ancestry. You might find one or more of these practices more helpful than others. Many of my friends and colleagues have used these practices to draw support from their lineage going back hundreds or even thousands of years. I find that going back beyond known ancestors has helped me expand my consciousness and discover resources that have deepened my connection to a greater web of support. I now feel this connection in my back as light energy, something I had never felt before. Time feels very different to me now; it has expanded into a web of interconnected energies and relationships from the past into the present and extending into the future. This ancestral web helps to hold me through life challenges. I feel part of a greater whole.

# PART THREE

# Developing Energetic Sovereignty

In part three, you will expand your ways of recognizing and working with Multidimensional Integrative Healing and learn about developing energetic sovereignty by learning practical methods for grounding, working with energies and creating healthy boundaries. You will also learn ways to work with energetic cords and how to connect more fully and expand into your True Self. Chapter 11 brings all of the practices together to show you what this looks like when applied in your life.

# 8

# Basic Tools for Energetic Sovereignty

Many of us find ourselves in situations where we feel depleted after interactions with other people. Our energy may be going out to them, and we may be absorbing their energy. If we are in a helping or teaching profession, or after a day of working with people, we may be exhausted and depleted. I recall many times after teaching when I would feel wrung out, emptied, and what I call "scary exhausted." Many of us too often report difficulties in family interactions where we lose ourselves or feel like we have taken on the problems of people close to us. In other situations, people in our life may be upset about something or have strong opinions that leave us worn out after interacting with them. The pandemic and lockdowns were especially problematic for many used to finding space from family members but who were then forced into spending long periods of time in close quarters with few options for creating boundaries and distance. During that time and afterward, many of us experienced anxiety, depression, and relationship difficulties. In addition, adult children may continue to live with their parents until marriage. Later, their parents may come to live with them in their later years. Maintaining energetic sovereignty while living near family members who are critical, abusive, and disrespectful of our life choices can be challenging.

The techniques in this chapter build on the resources you learned about earlier and provide ways to ground yourself, methods to assess where your energy is located, and ways to create boundaries and release unwanted energies. These simple techniques can make a big difference in how you live your life and tend your energy and boundaries.

## Why Energetic Sovereignty Is Important

Discovering that we can control and have agency over where our energy goes, what we allow into our energetic sphere, and what we do with the energy is life changing. We don't have to take in other people's energy. We also don't have to be aggressive or create a hard boundary in order to establish our energetic sovereignty. We can keep our hearts open and our empathy intact, and stay centered in ourselves. For many, just the idea that we have these choices makes a big difference. The tools and techniques offered here have helped many people live or interact with their difficult family members and be able to maintain their own boundaries. Sovereignty is about being aware of energy and making decisions about it rather than letting it happen to us.

The techniques that follow provide ways to ground yourself, methods to assess where your energy is located, and ways to create boundaries and release unwanted energies.

## Grounding Cord

Many of us find that we have a hard time being present. We may feel anxious, out of balance, and buffeted by the events of our times. Our minds may be busy bouncing from one thought to another, and we have difficulty centering ourselves or even settling our minds to begin meditation.

The grounding cord practice is an easy way to align with the present moment and connect to the energy of the earth. This simple exercise can be done whenever you wish to ground yourself. It can be incorporated into a daily practice before you meditate. You can do the grounding cord, call in your resources, and then begin meditation better supported and present.

When we do this exercise, we draw the energy of the earth up through a channel in the back of the body. Connecting to this energy straightens us up and anchors us to the earth, helping to create a sense of stabilization. This is especially helpful when we feel scattered or distracted. Connecting to the energy of the earth brings a sense of nourishment and energy to the nervous system.

### PRACTICE: GROUNDING CORD GUIDED IMAGERY SCRIPT

Before doing the grounding cord practice, it can be helpful to notice where your energy is. Take a moment, close your eyes, go inside, and notice where your energy is located. Do you find it in the computer screen, with a family member, or scattered and dispersed at a distance from your physical body? Is it extended far from you? Is it extending out from one side of you, or is it at a distance in front of you? Just the act of noticing where our energy is located is a good start to beginning energetic sovereignty.

After determining where your energy is, you can begin to call it back to you. You can simply ask that your energy return to you. You can use resource figures to help scoop it up and tuck it back in. Imagine calling the energy back in whatever way feels useful to you. For example, when I first did this, an image of hands came to me, and I imagined hands gathering up my energy and returning it to me. If it feels right, you can add bilateral stimulation as you do this exercise, tapping on your knees, drumming, or tapping either shoulder.

Close your eyes and go inside. Take a moment and feel yourself sitting. Sit up straight and feel your feet on the floor, your bottom on the seat. Notice where your energy is. If it is extended away from you, gently call it back. Imagine pulling any dispersed energy back to you.

When you feel your energy back, imagine energy pooling at the base of your spine. This is the place where your sit bones are. This triangle is at the base of your spine. Now imagine a root or a cord, made of anything you wish, going down deep into the earth. Going down, down, down through the earth layer. Imagine it going below the layer of earth that has been disturbed by human activity. Keep going down, further and further. Invite it to go down as far as it can, maybe even as far as the layer of rock. Take the time you need.

When you have gone as far down as you can, imagine bringing the earth energy back up through the cord. It comes up through the layers of rock, then dirt, until it reaches the base of your spine. Invite this energy to keep rising, drawing it up through the channel in your back. Imagine it going up, up, up beyond the base of your spine, into your lower back. Invite it to keep going up into your middle back. If you should sense that there is a block to the energy—this could be a feeling or even an image that comes to mind—imagine the earth energy going around that blockage and continuing up the channel in your back. Continue bringing this earth energy up. It goes into your upper back . . . then rises up into your neck . . . then into your head. Notice how that feels to be connected to the earth.

If you want, and if it feels right, you can imagine that earth energy going back down so that it's a two-way channel, going up and going down to connect it to the earth. Just take a moment and notice how that feels.

## Working with the Energy Bubble

The energy bubble is another way to take control of your energy and your boundaries. Since I've been using this exercise for myself and those I work with, I have found it to be a very helpful tool that is easy to learn and apply in life. The energy-bubble exercise is a way of recognizing energy surrounding our physical body, assessing energetic boundaries, taking control over them, and clearing energies that are unhelpful or unhealthy, or do not belong to us.

### Locating and Assessing the Energy Bubble

The energy bubble, in the shape of an egg, is transparent and surrounds our physical body. Some of us are able to see this bubble, while others can sense it. With this exercise we first determine the boundaries of our bubble, then call it back to us if it is misshapen or extended at a distance from us. We can mend any tears or holes in it. After doing these things, we examine the inside and exterior of our bubble to see if there are energies that don't belong to us there. If we determine there are, we clear these energies from our bubble by disinviting them or by calling in resource figures who can help us.

One of the things that I discovered when I did this exercise the first time was that in empathizing with other people, I tended to overlap my bubble with theirs. I realized that when I did that, I was merging with their energy in a way that wasn't good for me or them. I was taking their energy into my system, and it was draining me. When I realized that, I learned that I could call my energy bubble closer to me and allow the other person to contain their energy in their own energy bubble. From my bubble I could still feel empathy and attune to the other person without extending my bubble over theirs. That was revelatory for me.

I think this may be something that naturally empathic people do unknowingly with others they care about. We extend ourselves into their space to empathize. Instead, I now bring awareness to the pattern and consciously keep my energy bubble close to me, and I feel and attune to others from my separate space. If I find myself extending out to them, I can call my energy bubble back, and I can feel with them and empathize without overlapping with them.

## PRACTICE: LOCATING AND ASSESSING THE ENERGY BUBBLE

Close your eyes and go inside. Bring your attention inward. Take a moment to calm your mind. You might begin by calling your energy back, doing the grounding cord exercise, and tapping in your resource figures.

Invite a bubble of energy to surround you. It is transparent and in the shape of an egg. This bubble of energy represents your energetic sovereignty. The bubble should extend about one foot around your body but extends further to the front and sides and closer to your back. Notice the boundaries of your bubble. Locate the edges of it. How far does it extend?

Many of us do not "see" the bubble but access information from a sense or feeling. If that is true for you, to find it, you can start at the level of your skin and probe inch by inch until you have found where the edges are. Feel the size of your bubble.

Find the edges and the shape. Notice how it is in front. What shape is it? How is it in the back? How extended is it? Is it uniform like an egg? Or is it larger on one side or the other? Is it difficult to find because it is extended at a great distance from your body?

If it is misshapen or extended too far, you can call it back to you so that it is uniform in shape and closer to your physical body. You have control over this.

Examine the periphery of your bubble. See if there are any tears or openings in your bubble. If there are, imagine repairing them in whatever way feels good to you. For example, you can imagine mending the tears with sewing materials, bringing healing light to those places, or simply imagining them closing with your intention and compassionate awareness.

## Taking Control of the Bubble, Setting Boundaries

After collecting information about your energy bubble, you can decide what changes you might wish to make. Is it the way you want it?

- If it is extended way out, you can invite it to come back in.

- If you merge or overlap your bubble with certain people in your life and lose your boundaries, you can call your bubble back to yourself.

- If it is misshapen, you can reshape it by bringing awareness and imagining doing this.

- You can set rules for the energy bubble—what is allowed and what isn't. For example, you can set the rule that only your energy is allowed in your bubble; other people's energy is to remain outside. You can set a rule that you will not give energy away to others.

- If your bubble is extended over other people's bubbles, you can gently call it back in closer to you. You have control over the boundaries of your bubble.

You can bring awareness to your energy bubble when you're with friends, family, clients, or others. Notice what happens to it. Does it expand, contract, or merge with theirs? You can decide what feels right to you and call it back to you.

## Using Drawing to Assess and Reinforce Boundaries

You can use drawing to assess where your bubble is in relation to people with whom you have problematic relationships. Draw yourself in your bubble and the other person in theirs. Are the bubbles overlapping? What shape are they? Are there colors in the bubbles? Notice if there is an energy in your bubble that does not belong to you. This assessment can provide a lot of information about what might be causing difficulty in a relationship. If you are not comfortable with drawing, simple stick figures are sufficient.

You can also reinforce these boundaries by using art and writing. Visually represent yourself, and then draw a circle around yourself representing your energy bubble. Draw a picture of a person you have had difficulty setting boundaries with, and then draw a circle around them. Make sure that the circles are not overlapping. You can reinforce the boundary by writing the rules for the boundaries around the edges of the circle. These rules could include things such as "Their energy stays in their bubble, and mine in my bubble" and "I have a right to my boundaries and energetic sovereignty."

## Clearing Unwanted or Unwholesome Energies from Inside and Outside the Bubble

Some of us are very sensitive to other people's energy and are too permeable for our well-being. We can pick up the energy of our clients, family, friends, or even strangers. We can notice if there is anything in our bubble or adhering to the outside of it that doesn't belong to us. For example, our energy may be a certain color. Is there energy of another color in our bubble? We might sense a vibration different from ours. We can inquire: What is ours and what is not ours in our bubble? If you discover energy that isn't yours, you can inquire as to what it is and to whom it may belong.

We can ask ourselves, *Is this energy I discovered something I wish to keep in my bubble?* If the answer is "No it is not," you can choose to release it. There are many ways this can be done:

- You can imagine releasing it into light of any color that you wish and send it out into the universe where it belongs.

- You can imagine it going into the earth as compost.

- If you feel you need help releasing it from your bubble, you can call on a resource figure, such as a helping spirit, angelic being, or any figure that you sense would help with this task.

- How would you like to imagine releasing or cleansing your bubble of energies that do not belong to you? What imagery comes to you?

- If you wish, you can use bilateral stimulation, such as bilateral tapping, as you imagine doing these things.

## PRACTICE: CLEARING UNWANTED OR UNWHOLESOME ENERGIES FROM THE ENERGY BUBBLE

After locating the boundaries of your energy bubble, bring your attention to sense any energies that do not belong to you inside your bubble or even attached to the outside of it. If you see colors, you might notice a color or form inside your bubble that is not yours. Some people recognize their energy as having a particular color and notice energies of different colors inside their bubble that do not belong to them. If you do not "see" colors or shapes, you might be aware of the feeling of an energy or a vibration of something that is not yours.

If you discover energy that is not yours, ask what it is and whom it belongs to. Listen to what comes. Is this energy you wish to keep in your bubble? Remember, you have a right to your energetic sovereignty and do not have to hold anything that you do not wish to.

If you discover energies that are not yours and you wish to release them, ask yourself how you would like to do that. You can imagine them leaving your bubble and ascending into light of any color. You can imagine the energies being composted as nourishment for the land. You can call on any resources to help you, including those you have tapped in as your team or any others that come to mind, to assist in this endeavor. If you wish, you can tap right-left, right-left as you imagine doing these things.

For psychotherapists or others in the healing professions, you can use this same method for clearing your bubbles after sessions. If you feel that you have your clients' energies in your bubble, you can release it into light, imagine composting it into the earth, or invite resource figures to help in the clearing work. You can tap yourself as you imagine these things.

## Energetic Cleansing

There are times when we feel drained, even burdened, but don't know why. It might be after spending time with a large group of people, visiting a city, or engaging with family members who are conflictual. I've even had this feeling after sleeping in a hotel room. It may be that you have picked up energies from these places or people that don't belong to you. If you notice that there are energies that are not yours, there are methods to clear these energies. For many years I have taught in retreat or workshop settings where there are large groups of people doing intensive personal work. Often I would find myself exhausted and feeling like I was carrying energies that were not mine. It's hard to describe this, but for me it felt like a coating on the outside of my body—I felt emotionally sapped, burdened, and heavyhearted. Several times I sought out energy healers who helped to release these energies that I had picked up from the environment. Even though the retreat places were wonderful and the work that was being done there beneficial, a lot of energy was being released, and it seemed to stick to me. After the energy-clearing work with these healers, I felt back to myself, my vitality recovered, yet I knew I needed tools for release and protection.

Energetic cleansing can be performed prior to spiritual practice or ritual or after recognizing that you are carrying energies that are not yours. Indigenous cultures throughout the world recognize the need for energetic cleansing. Though these cultures are rooted in different parts of the world, many of the methods used are similar. Indigenous peoples of North America—including the Navajo, Dakota, Chumash, Lakota, Ojibwe, Anishinaabe, and First Nations communities—use sage as part of energetic cleansing. Bundled dried sage leaves are burned and the smoke is used for "smudging," which is believed to dispel negative energy and purify a space, person, or object. This cleansing helps to promote spiritual balance and harmony. Many cultures include immersion in water as a cleansing ritual. Ritual cleansing is rooted in ancient practices performed throughout history worldwide. Christian baptism has its roots in the Jewish tradition of purification that involves washing or immersing in water. You might be familiar with how you feel after taking a shower following a long day. Beyond feeling physically clean, you feel refreshed, the troubles from your day washed away.

When I was in the Andes and Amazon Basin of Ecuador, a group of us participated in several cleansing rituals. These rituals were done to prepare our group for our entrance into the Sacred Headwaters of the Amazon and the journey we were embarking on with the Sapara people. In the Andes we met with a curandera, or traditional healer. The women in our group were separated from the men. Each group met with the curandera in a cinder-block room with a dirt floor; two children tended a small fire. The group of women sat on the ground in a circle while one by one we were called on to remove our clothing to our underwear and receive the cleansing ritual. While chanting softly, the curandera gently brushed our bodies with sacred plants tied in a bundle she had collected from the nearby mountains. She blew tobacco smoke on us and sprayed us with liquid from her mouth that was made from sacred plants. She also passed an egg over our bodies.

Later, when our group arrived on a tiny airstrip in the middle of the Amazon rainforest, the shaman Manari Ushigua and men, women, and children from his village welcomed us and then performed ritual cleansing, much like the curandera had done, involving tobacco smoke and brushing our bodies with plants. This also included inhaling through each nostril liquid tobacco, which gave us a head rush and tears. After the cleansing, our faces were painted with pigments from local plants. We were also invited to bathe in the river, which completed the cleansing, before we entered the sacred grounds where the teaching and work with the shaman would take place. I understood that our group coming from the city and our busy lives needed to be cleansed of those energies before coming into their space. In that way we would not bring those energies with us. We would enter the home of the Indigenous people cleanly.

When I imagine energetic cleansing, I recall the feeling of being brushed by the plants the curandera and shaman used. I can recall the sense of being cleansed of energetic contaminants and bring that feeling into the present with imagined cleansing. For me, imagining the brushing, tobacco smoke, and immersion in the river work well.

You can imagine cleansing yourself in whatever way works for you. You might imagine standing under a waterfall with pure, clean water; immersing yourself in the sea, calling in spiritual resources to help clear energies; or being carefully brushed with healing plants. Sometimes just asking that any energies that don't belong to you be disinvited works well.

## The Energetic Containment Room

There are times when situations arise in our lives that hijack our minds, causing us to ruminate, worry, and loop in the same thoughts, feelings, and even conversations. Often these situations have no obvious solution, but our minds keep returning. This can take up much of the space in our minds, leaving little room for constructive thoughts or creativity. It is as if all the energy is being siphoned off into unproductive circling thoughts and feelings. This is what I experienced when my mother passed away and her vaguely worded will created chaos in my family.

## My Experience with the Energetic Containment Room

With the anarchy that ensued with the settlement of my mother's estate, I found my mind cycling with upsetting thoughts and strong feelings of anger, hurt, resentment, and betrayal. It felt like an invasion of undesirable energies into my personal space. I awakened in the morning with these thoughts and went to sleep with them. When I sat in meditation, my mind was distracted by them. It was as if my personal space was now occupied by these noxious energies, leaving little room for focus on the things that were important to me.

I explained to my mentor Jean Schneider what was occurring in my life and the trouble I was having with these intrusive energies. She suggested we create an "energetic containment room"—a room that can hold and contain all these energies I did not wish to have in my space. First, she told me to identify what exactly I was dedicating the space to and to find precise words to describe it. This is a room or a space that is for a particular purpose. All the components that are related to it are represented in the room. What we take into the room is now independent of the rest of our life.

I needed a room that could contain the negative energies that were specifically associated with decisions around the contents of my mother's house. We worked to come up with a title for the room that was specific to its role. I came up with "a room for probate of the contents of my mother's house." I then closed my eyes, went inside, and asked for an image to form that represented such a room. What came to me was a courtroom. I then asked what I needed in the room. What came was a sense of justice, rules, truth, fairness; a judge who would set the rules and that there would be no secrets. Everything would be done in an orderly fashion. I imagined a judge in a black robe seated at the front who represented justice. The executor and estate lawyer were seated to the left and problematic family members and their lawyers to the right. It was relieving to have all of this contained in this room with a judge in charge.

Jean told me to imagine a door to the room. At first I couldn't imagine a door, but then I saw a massive double oak door. Jean said it was important to imagine leaving the room and closing the door. I imagined doing that, then going down a hall and down in an elevator, getting into my car, and driving two hours home. In doing so, it felt like I had left the problems of my mother's estate and the related chaos far away. She told me I could enter and leave the room when I wished. If my mind took me unbidden to upsetting thoughts or feelings, I could remember the room and leave them there. They could be contained and taken care of there. I needed to remember to do this so that I could reclaim my energetic sovereignty and control over my inner space.

In the days after I did this exercise, I noticed a big change. I no longer ruminated on the thoughts about that situation or was activated by feelings about it. When my mind was taken by some thoughts, I quickly reminded myself that it was all in the room and I didn't need to concern myself with it. I saw in my mind's eye the courtroom with the judge and the others in it. I didn't need to be there. It was being taken care of. I had space in my mind to focus on the work and projects that were important to me and to my life in the present.

## Case of a Traumatized Man from a War-Torn Country

John had considerable war trauma that was causing him to be triggered and severely dysregulated. Despite his safety in this country, he still felt like he was back in a war zone. His therapist asked him if he would like to create a room where he could leave all the trauma from the war. He closed his eyes and went into a relaxed state and created a room that was made of metal, like a gigantic container with a door with hinges and a big lock. It was located on a military base. She asked if he would like to bring in anyone or anything to guard the door. He came up with ancient warriors from his ancestry as guardians. He also placed the room in the country where the war had taken place, far from where he now lived. He imagined leaving all the things that had happened in the war and the trauma in that room, closing the door with the warriors guarding it, then flying back to the US, leaving it all in that space. He did all this imagining while tapping on either shoulder. After he was through, he opened his eyes and had a big smile on his face. He was noticeably calmer and relaxed.

## Using the Energetic Containment Room with Medical Concerns and Pain Management

The energetic containment room can be used for medical concerns and even pain management. A room can be created that can hold worries, concerns, and even pain. It can be made of anything the person imagines that would be helpful. Resources can be brought into the room to help. What is needed here?

Monica was having intrusive thoughts about a recently diagnosed medical condition. Some of them were self-blaming and harsh. Her therapist suggested the energetic containment room exercise: "Imagine a room where you can put all your thoughts and worries about this medical situation." She came up with a detailed dedication that explained what the room was for and a description of the room. She closed her eyes, went inside, and, using bilateral stimulation (pulsars), waited for an image to arise that represented the desired space. She imagined a blue room. It had an old wooden door with carved figures on it. She imagined her ancestors as guardians of the door. After leaving these worries and negative thoughts inside, she closed the door and left. She felt relieved afterward, much better than she had before the exercise. She knew that if the thoughts returned, she could remember to leave them in the blue room where they could be contained.

What follows is a script that you can use to create an energetic containment room. You might want to use this if you are ruminating or worrying about a situation, to help you put the situation aside and work on it when you wish, rather than have it take up room in your mind.

## PRACTICE: STEPS FOR CREATING AN ENERGETIC CONTAINMENT ROOM

Think about a situation you find yourself in that is troubling you but does not require your attention currently. It could be a problem at home or work or with family, a situation regarding your health, trauma from the past, or even something that is happening politically that does not require your attention all the time. You can create an energetic containment room where you can place all of the thoughts, worries, and even resources that can help there.

Decide what purpose the space will serve. What is it you are dedicating the space to? Find precise words to describe it. This is a room or a space that is for a particular purpose. Give the room a title that is specific to its role—for example, "This room is to hold all my worries about my health."

Close your eyes and go inside. Take a few moments to settle and center yourself. Ask for an image to form that represents such a room. You can tap, rattle, drum, or use any kind of bilateral stimulation if it helps with this.

Ask for a door that opens into this room. Notice what the door looks like. It can be made of anything you wish. It is important to have a door to this room, as this allows you to enter and leave the room, closing the door, as you wish. If you desire, you can imagine guardians at the door.

Now enter the room. What would you like represented here? What is needed in the room? See what comes to mind. What do you want to take into this room? What you take into the room is now independent of the rest of your life. Art can be used to enhance the space. You can paint or draw the space to reinforce it.

Spend as much time as you need to create the room and leave anything that you don't wish to take with you in there. When you are ready to leave, imagine opening the door, departing the space, and closing the door behind you. If you wish, you can keep guardians there for added protection.

Later, if your mind takes you unbidden to upsetting thoughts or feelings, you can remember the room and leave them there.

## Summary

### *Taking Charge of Your Energetic Sovereignty*

In this chapter you learned about energetic sovereignty, ways to take charge of your boundaries, and methods for releasing energies that are not yours. You learned about energy clearing, the grounding cord, the energy bubble, and the energetic containment room. All of these tools can be used as part of a regular practice to help maintain your boundaries and keep you feeling clear in your own field of energy. The notion that you don't need to carry other people's energies in order to be a caring, compassionate person may change your relationship to yourself and others in your life. In the next chapter you will learn another way to manage energies that flow from one person to another through energetic pathways.

# 9

# Working with Energetic Cords

There are times when we experience difficulties in relationships because we are having trouble creating healthy boundaries with people in our life. We may feel that we are taking in unwholesome messages or negative emotions that are affecting us. We may even have problems discerning what is ours and what is coming from someone else. An example might be a woman living with her mother, who is very critical. She repeatedly tells her daughter she isn't pretty, smart, or capable. She repeats these things with an angry look on her face. The daughter tries her best to not absorb these negative messages, yet she knows they are getting into her. She cannot get away from her mother physically because she lives with her and cannot afford to move out. She also feels guilty about trying to defend herself and the anger she feels from the attacks. She struggles to maintain her personal energetic sovereignty.

Energetic cords are invisible energetic pathways between one person and another person, a person and a place, or a person and ancestors that transfer energy, information, and emotions that can be helpful or harmful. When we check up inside, we can feel places in our body where these energetic cords are attaching to us. These energetic pathways hold contracts, agreements, and history. In our work to develop energetic sovereignty and boundaries, assessing and understanding where these attachments might be and what information is passing through them is helpful. After gathering information about the energetic attachments, we can then decide what is best to do. We have control over what information we want to allow through the cords and where we want them attached. This is a powerful idea that has transformed and changed many people's lives and their relationships with people close to them.

## Assessing the Cords and Attachments

When we suspect we may have unwholesome cords attached to us from another person, we can explore and gather information about them that can then guide our work. You can begin by scanning the front of your body and paying attention to any sensation in your body where the cord or cords might be. You can scan your back too. Most cords are in the front. What is the color, shape, texture of the cord? What is the attachment place like? Where does the attachment point end—on the surface of the body or deep inside? How is it attached? Are there hooks? Do the cords go all the way to the back, or are they on the surface? Is there more than one? Be curious in your exploration and inquiry.

It can be helpful to draw a sketch of yourself showing where the cords are attached to you from the person you are concerned about. The cords can take many different forms. For some people and relationships, they may be thick and very tough; other times, they may be like tendrils or webs. The cords may take the form of light or energies that flow from one person to another.

After asking what the cords look like and where they are attached, you want to inquire about what is going through the cord. What kind of energy, messages, emotions? Maybe it is the message of "You're not good enough," "You're not worthy of love," or "You're not safe." The energy going through the cord may be dark and dense, sticky like tar, or red and fiery. You might use your sensate faculty to feel into where you have the attachments and what the qualities and messages might be. You can draw stick-figure representations of yourself and where you are sensing the attachments. This can be helpful in the assessment.

## Setting Rules for the Cords

After your assessment of the cords and the attachments, you can decide what changes you wish to make to these cords. What do you want to allow through your cord? What do you not wish to allow to come through? Pose these questions to the cord and listen to an inner knowing.

For example, in the above case, the daughter senses a thick cord from her heart to her mother that has dark energy. The rules might be *I only want information that is useful to me—nothing that is critical or hurtful is allowed.*

## Create a Compost Cord

You can create a compost cord. When there is unwholesome energy and messages that you don't want to come through the cord, you can create a cord that branches out from the main cord and goes into the earth to compost this information. The earth can then use this energy as nourishment to feed life. Would you like to imagine a cord that branches from the main one and takes any unwanted energies, messages, or emotions into the earth for composting?

In this way you will not take in any undesirable energies. If the idea of a composting cord does not appeal to you, you can create any imagery that works for you to manage the energies you don't desire. For example, you might imagine healing light from a spiritual source or other images from nature.

### Cutting or Releasing Cords

Sometimes the energies and messages are too negative to be affected by rules or composting. In these cases, you may wish to cut the cords. How would you like to imagine doing this? Would you like to bring in help? Perhaps a spiritual resource figure might be called upon to help, such as archangel Michael, one of your helping spirits, or other resource figures. Ask yourself, *What do I need to release these cords? What do I need to cut them?* Wait to see what comes up for you. An image may appear immediately, such as a sharp blade or a figure that comes to help you. Sometimes the cords are dissolved, not cut. You may want to do this a little bit at a time, as it can be too much of a change for the system. Some people experience a significant detoxification after cutting cords, including sweating and gastrointestinal releases. It may also be important not to think about the other person or give them energy for a set period of time. In this way, the old energetic pathway is not reasserted, and you can heal.

The idea of cutting cords may not resonate with you. It may feel too violent for you, or you may wish to release the connection in a different way. How would you like to imagine releasing the cord in a way that feels right to you? It is always best to explore what is in the way and what you need rather than push for a result. Perhaps there is an honoring of the attachment or some kind of ritual is required. Maybe you wish to bring in resources for the person you are corded to. For example, in the case of the mother who was sending critical messages to her daughter, the daughter may wish to imagine bringing in a compassionate angelic being to provide her mother the love and care that she is lacking. When this has been imagined, she can then release the cord to her mother.

After cutting or releasing the cord, you may want to bring in some kind of healing imagery to the places where the cords had been attached. Some people like to imagine a liquid blue blessing field or light flowing to the places, while others may imagine golden healing light emanating from a divine source. I ask my clients if they would like to imagine bringing healing imagery to the places where the cords had been attached. Whatever imagery or even sense of healing that arises for you is fine. You can use bilateral stimulation to help with the integration of the imagery if you wish.

## PRACTICE: STEPS FOR WORKING WITH ENERGETIC CORDS

The following is a script that can help you locate where you might have cords attached and suggestions for working with them.

Close your eyes and go inside. Take a few moments to settle yourself. Begin by thinking of the person you suspect you might be attached to through energetic cords. As you think of them, what do you notice in your body? Mentally scan the surface of your body, and even deeper, exploring where there might be attachments. Where do you notice the energetic attachment points? How deep do these cords go? What is the consistency of the cord? Is it thick, thin, fibrous? If there is more than one cord, examine each one. What does it feel like? What are the messages, beliefs, emotions that are passing through the cord? Is there a color, temperature, or form to the attachments? Write down what these things are. You can draw a diagram of your body and indicate where the cords are attached. At this time, if you wish, you can begin bilateral stimulation.

Now as you tune in to the information that is coming through the cords, you can decide what you want to allow to be transmitted and what you want to disallow. You can set rules for the energies and messages passing through the cords. For example, you can set a rule that only information that is supportive and helpful for you can come through the cord; anything that is harmful or hurtful is not allowed. Instead of blocking the negative information from coming through the cord to you, you can create a new cord that branches out from the main one and carries the negative energies and harmful messages into the earth to be composted. Do you wish to compost some of the negative energies? If so, you can imagine a cord going into the earth carrying these energies as nourishment for the earth.

If you discover that the information coming through the cord is too negative and the energy or messages are not responding to the rule setting and composting cord, you might decide to cut the cord or cords. If you wish to cut the cords, how would you like to imagine that? What do you need to accomplish that? Do you need help? You can bring in one of the resource figures that you tapped in before or bring in a spiritual resource that is a better fit for this job.

After cutting the cord or cords, imagine bringing healing to the places where the cords were attached. You might invite in imagery of a liquid blue blessing field or any imagery that feels right for you.

Check in with yourself to see how you feel and if the cords have reattached themselves. Sometimes the cords reattach, and the cord cutting and rule setting need to be redone. You can reinforce the rules you set for the cords once a day by saying the words out loud or writing them down.

## Examples of Cord Work

Olivia described a troubling situation with her mother, who was talking about her behind her back with other family members, attacking her, and undermining her. Olivia was emotionally distressed. She described that her mother had always had an ambivalent relationship with her that was upsetting and at times created significant confusion and anxiety. She believed this was a pattern—mothers loving and hurting their daughters—in the family line.

When she closed her eyes and went inside, she located the cord to her mother around the base of her spine, her root chakra—the area that corresponded to survival. This made sense to her. In the past, though she was a competent and independent adult woman, she felt panic and even dissociated thinking about separating from her mother. After exploring what felt best to do, she decided that it would be best to cut this cord, as it was not serving her. However, before doing this, she wanted to communicate to her mother through the cord all her love and appreciation for her life. She sent her gratitude for the support her mother had given her and all the good things that she had received from her.

After sending love and gratitude through the cord to her mother, she was ready to cut the cord. She immediately sensed difficulty cutting it herself, as it was very thick and fibrous. When asked what help she needed to accomplish this, the archangel Michael—though not one of her previously tapped-in resources—immediately came to mind. He appeared luminous, compassionate, with a sword in hand. He easily cut the thick cord attached at her root chakra with his sword. When this was accomplished, Olivia felt relief, freedom from the binding to her mother. She noted that there was a space where the cord had attached, and she wished to send healing to that space. She imagined liquid blue light from the blessing field filling the spaces where the cord and filaments had been, healing and soothing. After that, she imagined the light going down into the earth, then up through all her chakras and through the top of her head, which created a free flow of energy. This process felt healing, even elating.

After this session, Olivia felt huge relief. The anxiety she felt was gone. For a while she limited contact with her mother and focused on her own healing. Over time, her relationship with her mother transformed. Her mother ceased sending toxic, hurtful energy her way. Now, instead, there is a feeling of love and gratitude that flows between them that is comfortable and easeful.

In another example, Elaine was being emotionally and mentally attacked with chaotic, hurtful messages by a family member. She felt poisoned by the assaults and didn't know how to protect herself. When she closed her eyes and went inside to explore where the cords might be, she reported that they felt like slimy, poisonous webs all over her back, like jellyfish tentacles. There were many of them. She wanted to get rid of them, as they were painful and very toxic. When she explored what she needed to clean them off, an image of a kind of scraper came to mind, like a tool used to scrape snow and ice from a windshield. It seemed instead of cutting them, she would scrape them off. She closed her eyes and imagined doing this. It took some time to clean them off. Because she knew that the attacks on her would most likely continue from this disturbed person, she decided she needed a protective shield that was made of mirrors erected around her to reflect anything coming from the family member. But to create this shield, she needed help. When she explored what she needed, she decided to bring in helping spirits or guardians to erect it and make sure it was in place. She took several minutes imagining this help coming in, creating, and setting up the protective shield. She especially needed protection from the back, as this was where most of the attacks from this person were going. An expiration date of two months was set for the shield, as it wasn't advised to keep this up indefinitely.

She determined not to think about, talk about, or send any negative thoughts or energy to the disturbed family member. In this way she would not send any of her energy to that person and could begin to become invisible to them, and not a target. She continued to do the grounding cord practice with a cord going into the earth in daily meditation and to bring liquid blue healing light into the area where the toxic cords were removed. After this session she reported feeling better. The attacks on her ceased. Two years later she was able to have a guarded but psychically safe relationship with the family member.

## Working with Energetic Cords from the Ancestral Lineage

Ancestral cords are energetic pathways that flow between our genetic and spiritual ancestors and ourselves. These energetic pathways hold contracts, agreements, and history. These cords can be worked with so that we can make changes to the contracts, old beliefs, and unwholesome patterns. We can choose what we carry forward in our ancestral lineage. What do you want to bring forward through your lineage? What do you want to let go of? These energetic attachments can be felt in our body. We can choose what we allow and do not allow in. We can create rules that we apply to the cords. With the rules we can invite wholesome energy to flow through. We can also send the unwholesome, unhelpful information through a cord that goes into the earth as compost or one that brings healing light. We want to hold our lineage with compassion.

We all have people in our ancestry who have qualities that we admire and those who do not. We all have perpetrators as well as victims. We also share the energy we carry with other people, especially those close to us, such as our children. This is recognized as the mirror neuron system, whereby the emotional state in the parent or caregiver is felt or mirrored in the child's developing nervous system through a kind of unconscious empathic resonance. Working with the energetic cords, we can choose to let go of information that is unhealthy and open the pathways to let in what is healthy and beneficial.

In working with ancestral cords, you want to begin by quieting your thinking mind and then setting your intention. What are the old beliefs, patterns, and energies that have been passed down in your lineage that you wish to purge? Next, you scan your body as you think about these old messages and see where they may be attached to you in the form of energetic pathways. Where on your body are these cords attached? What do they consist of? Some are dense and thick like well-traveled roads, and others are less pronounced. What are the energies, messages, and limiting beliefs that are traveling down these pathways? Next, you want to determine what you want to keep. For example, you might wish to keep the strength and determination of your lineage. You may also want to determine what you wish to prevent from coming through your lineage. There are many ways to do this, including sending the messages or energies to divine light, composting them, and setting rules for the cords about what you want to let through and what you wish to prevent from coming through.

## PRACTICE: WORKING WITH ANCESTRAL CORDS OR ENERGETIC PATTERNS

Close your eyes and go inside. Bring your attention inward. Take a moment to calm your mind. You might begin by calling your energy back, do the grounding cord exercise, and tap in your resource figures.

The purpose of this practice is to discover where there are attachments to old unwholesome patterns from your lineage and to let go of anything that is not serving you. You can also work with a particular energetic attachment from a person in your ancestry.

Take a moment and scan your body to find where you feel the connection to old lineage patterns in your body. Where are the energetic attachment points located on your body? What do the cords look like? Are they thick, thin, strong, or weak? Is there a color, temperature, vibration, or form to the attachments? What are the messages, beliefs, limitations, and energy they carry? You can draw a diagram of your body and illustrate where the cords are attached and what they look like. Write down what you discover.

What do you want to keep from your lineage? Which of the energies, messages, and qualities would you like to allow in? When you can feel the quality or the feeling from the ancestor or lineage you wish to invite in, you can add bilateral stimulation if you want.

What do you want to let go of that is not serving you? Light of any color you wish can be sent to these energies or messages to help heal or help them. They can also be sent to the earth to be composted. You can also set rules for what is allowed through the cords and what is not.

## Setting Rules for the Cords

What follows are some rules you can set for the cords that can help turn on or turn off the flow of information from the lineage.

- You can ask for the connection to the ancestral trauma to be turned off or disconnected.

- You can make rules about how much of a connection you want to any of the ancestral energy.

- You can turn down the volume or intensity of ancestral trauma energy.

- You can put rules on the cord: for example, *Only information that is wise and healthy for me* or *Only information that can keep me safe*, and so forth.

- You can turn off the conduit to ancestral trauma and open it when you want to work on it, targeting it with EMDR or directly bringing resources to it.

- You can ask for an energetic conduit to open for the flow of wholesome energy and information.

- You can imagine anything that is not wholesome being channeled into the earth as compost or going to a source of light.

- It is important to hold these old patterns and energies with compassion. Let them know that they are no longer needed or helpful to you.

## Working with Blocks to Releasing Ancestral Traumas and Unwholesome Patterns

Sometimes when we begin to release ancestral traumas or unwholesome patterns, we experience blocks to letting these things go. It is as if a voice in our mind says, *No, you can't let this go. You need it*. Maybe fear comes up, or even guilt, and you don't know why. Where is this coming from? It is helpful to explore these blocks with an open mind. What is this about? Where did this come from? What are the limiting beliefs? Sometimes there are issues of loyalty that compel us to carry ancestral traumas in our lives and into our families. It may not feel okay to release these messages and energetic patterns. If you feel it is not, then ask yourself, *Why not?* Are these things necessary today, or are they vestiges from what was needed in earlier times for survival? Is it helpful to your loved ones now if you are worried and fearful all the time? Is this helping your ancestors?

I believe we can honor the traumas from the past and even name them without carrying them in our body-minds and passing them on to our children and grandchildren. I believe the idea of honor and respect without carrying the traumas is very important. We can keep the lessons without keeping the trauma. What happens when you imagine doing these things? What are the blocks? What are the unspoken agreements or contracts? You can explore these blocks and then challenge them with Socratic questions or bring in resource figures to help or give advice.

## Example of Ancestral Healing in My Lineage

In my lineage I can find stories and information that go back many generations, especially on my father's side of the family. I have never felt particularly inspired by these ancestors, even though the women in my family were very strong. The reason I did not feel a connection to them was because even though they were strong women who overcame tremendous obstacles in their lives, they were not kind people. My father's mother was cold, as were both of my great-grandmothers on my father's side. I did not want to emulate strength that lacked caring for others. What I have come to understand is that we can connect to the healthy part of our ancestry—the part that we wish to draw inspiration and strength from—without taking in all of the other characteristics these people also carried. When we work with cords—these energetic pathways between people and places—we can choose what we wish to allow in and what we want to keep out. This idea was revelatory for me.

I could connect to the strength and fortitude of my female ancestors, including my great-grandmothers, without taking in their coldness and even their cruelty.

In the early 1900s, my paternal great-grandmother Martha Belle Buckley Parnell traveled with six children in a covered wagon from Boone County, Arkansas, to Ochiltree, Texas, a desolate place in the Texas panhandle, where they settled and she raised her family alone. On the way there, in 1902, her husband, Lowrey Parnell, died. This journey took several years during which Martha and her children worked on farms to earn enough money to survive and to allow them to continue westward.

This woman was hard. She was so hard that two of her sons never married but lived together in a shack, using the same bed they slept on in the wagon. As the family story goes, their only sister, Esther Ollie, hated the isolated life on that ranch, "went crazy," and was placed in an institution in Taneyville, Missouri, where she spent the rest of her life.

My other paternal great-grandmother, Millie, was also a formidable woman. When she was sixty-one, she and her husband, Charlie, moved to a remote mountainous area in Trinity County, in northern California, carrying backpacks several hours on a bluff trail to reach the homestead. There they built a simple wood cabin with a Buck stove and lived off the land. Millie was a tough, no-nonsense woman who carried a long gun and stared you in the eye. After Charlie's death in his eighties. she continued to live in the isolated homestead into her late eighties, until it became too much for her to manage alone. My father and grandmother helped move her to a cabin down a long dirt road still many miles from the nearest town.

I have always admired the strength of my great-grandmother Millie, whom I had met a couple of times, but she was so cold and tough I could never relate to her. She seemed to care little for her children or grandchildren. Like my father's other grandmother (whom he never met), she was tough and unfriendly.

I would like to imagine connecting with these ancestral women energetically and opening a channel that can allow the qualities that are helpful and resourceful for me to flow from them to me. At the same time, I can set a rule that prevents any cold, misanthropic energy or unwholesome ancestral patterns from passing through the cord to me. I can choose what I invite into my system and what I bring forward into life. I can imagine this old pattern that both of my great-grandmothers carried of cold toughness and isolation from society going into the earth as replenishment and compost. I can imagine doing this with compassion.

If I were to make a list of the qualities or energetic patterns that are helpful to me from my great-grandmothers Martha Belle and Millie, they are physical and mental strength; resourcefulness; power; a no-nonsense, can-do attitude; adventurousness; courageousness; endurance; and fortitude. They thought differently, were outliers, and were connected to the land. Both were able to leave their homes and venture into the unknown and make their lives.

When I imagine my great-grandmothers Martha Belle and Millie and their qualities I want to allow in, I feel it in my hands, throat, and back. I imagine opening the conduit to this resourceful energy and allowing it to flow into me. I take in the good things, feel them, and honor those qualities. I also acknowledge what isn't helpful and imagine those things being composted with compassion into the earth.

## Summary

### *Energetic Cords: Assessing Attachments and Taking Control over How You Wish to Manage Them*

In this chapter you learned about energetic cords—energetic pathways that hold contracts, agreements, and history—and ways to work with them so that you can take control over the information that is passing through them to you. I outlined assessing where cords are attached, what they consist of, and how you want to manage them. Not only do we have cords attached to living people but also to ancestors and our lineages. We also have control over that information so that we don't allow what is not wholesome or helpful to pass from them to us or to future generations.

In the next chapter you will learn about the True Self and how to connect with and align with this essential part of yourself so that you can live more fully and authentically.

# 10

# Working with the True Self

One of the most important resources that we have is the one that is closest to us—our True Self. Your True Self is the blueprint of who you are, your unique expression that is whole and complete. This is the deepest part of you: your essence, a core of goodness that has been there since the moment of conception, or before. This part has never been touched by any of the bad things that have happened in your life. It is the part of you that has a drive toward wholeness and recognizes when you have veered off a healthy life path. When we align with our True Self, we can identify those things that are not authentic, such as energetic patterns, belief systems that falsely define us, or things we have attached to us that are not ours. In this chapter we'll look at ways to explore blocks to True Self as well as methods for working with them in a variety of ways.

Many people recognize the True Self at the end of an EMDR session. I remember a woman telling me, after processing an incident of childhood sexual abuse, that what happened to her did not define who she was and that it had never touched her essential self.

She recognized that her True Self was there all along but had been obscured by the emotional damage done by the perpetrator. After EMDR, she felt free and alive in a way she had not experienced before. Many describe how they felt after an EMDR session like a cleansing, and they felt a free flow of energy through their bodies where before there had been blocks.

Though many discover a strong felt sense of their True Self at the conclusion of an EMDR session, you can use the following practice to contact it. You can enhance it by tapping right-left, right-left on the sides of your legs; crossing your arms and tapping either shoulder; or using any kind of bilateral stimulation you choose. When you discover a sense of your True Self, you can invite the feeling to expand into your entire body. Allow it to fill in all the spaces inside, through your core and into your limbs, organs, skin, and cells. Feel the free flow of energy as you fill into your True Self.

### PRACTICE: TAPPING IN THE TRUE SELF

Close your eyes and go inside. Feel yourself sitting. Take some deep breaths in and slowly let them out. Relax and let go with the exhalation.

Take another deep breath, breathing up from the center of the earth, filling yourself with breath; then release your breath back down into the earth. Let go of all the tension in your body and mind as you exhale. Take some more deep breaths, relaxing with the exhalations.

When you feel relaxed, imagine going to your Peaceful Place. Take as much time as you need to go there. Open your senses and feel yourself in your special place. If you like, you can tap right-left, right-left a few times to increase the feeling.

Now ask to connect to your True Self. This essential part of yourself was there before you were born and has been there all of your life. This is the part of you that has been with you through all you have experienced in your life yet has not been touched by any of it. This part of you is pure, good, innocent, wise, and resilient. It is the unique blueprint of your life expression. This is the core of your being. When you find a sense of it, even a glimmer, invite the energy of your True Self to begin to expand. If you would like to, and it feels right for you, tap as you imagine this expansion of your True Self into all of the places in your body. It might begin in your heart, then radiate out into your other organs, your limbs, all the cells of your body. Your True Self energy might have a color—notice that. Let it fill you. Notice, too, any places that feel blocked or energy of a different color that does not belong to you. If you notice any energies that are not yours, you can kindly invite them to leave your space and go where they need to go. As you invite your True Self energy to fill you, notice how this feels. Recognize this essential self, as it will help you to notice when you are not acting from this self or if there is something that needs tending.

Remember, your True Self is always with you. You can contact it whenever you need to.

## Exploring Blocks to True Self and What Does Not Belong

Sometimes we have difficulty finding our True Self. If you have difficulty accessing and aligning with your True Self, explore what the blockages are. Ask yourself, *What is blocking this connection?* Then wait for an answer to come from your inner knowing. It might be a dark energy, a constriction in a part of your body, or old beliefs that prohibit this. For example, one woman whom I guided in this exercise felt a block to her True Self like a closed door or wall. Upon inquiring what it might be, she discovered the spirit of a deceased person had attached to her and needed help. (This is described more fully in chapter 15.) These blockages can be addressed and worked with in a variety of ways, including with energy cleansing, calling in helping spirits or other resource figures, the use of imagery, or EMDR targeting and reprocessing memories from the past that might be linked. When these things are cleared, often you will feel in alignment with your True Self, which you can later access more easily.

Sometimes after connecting with your True Self, you are better able to notice energies that do not belong to you. These energies may not have blocked you from accessing your True Self, but you can sense that they are not yours. Using curious, compassionate inquiry, you can begin to explore what these things might be. Ask questions and listen, see what is discovered. When doing inquiry, you want to suspend your concepts and beliefs and notice what arises freshly. This is where a meditation practice to quiet your mind and listen is helpful. Nonjudgmental awareness is essential because often what arises doesn't make sense to the thinking mind yet is meaningful and contains information worth exploring.

## Advice for Therapists and Healers

When working with people in healing work, it is important for therapists to compassionately resonate with their clients in a way that their clients can feel and respond to in kind. When healers align with their client's True Self, their clients feel seen, and this opens trust and reduces fear of the unknown. Together therapist and client can explore what is. When blocks to the True Self are identified, therapists and healers can use strategies such as EMDR focusing on the blocks to True Self for healing, clearing, and returning to the True Self. Origins of emotional or psychological blocks may link to the historical past, past lives, or even what is carried from other family members or ancestors. When these links are discovered, they can be targeted and reprocessed with EMDR or other methods for energy clearing.

For example, a client arrived for a session in a distressed state, with panic and anxiety after a visit with her family. Despite her emotional turbulence, because I knew her well, I could attune to her True Self and help her settle and remember herself. My seeing and attuning to her True Self enabled her to return to herself. We were then able to do EMDR on the roots of her distress.

## Example EMDR Session and Discovering the True Self

EMDR is a powerful therapy for clearing trauma, but it also helps us access and return to our True Self. Who we are when the conditioning is cleared is loving, luminous, and joyful. We feel our good heart.

This experience of recognition of True Self was beautifully expressed at the conclusion of an EMDR demonstration session by a man from my EMDR training. The "client" was a therapist who had worked for years on healing the severe neglect and physical and sexual abuse from his childhood. In this session, we had successfully completed the processing of incidents where he was sexually abused by a group of children and an incident where he was molested by a camp director, when he spontaneously experienced the purity of his True Self and an expanded feeling of self-love. He was luminous, so filled with love that everyone in the class could feel it in the room. Many, including myself, were moved to tears. We witnessed him recognize his True Self, the part of him that had never been touched by what had happened to him.

At the end of the session he imagined speaking to the camp director and correctly assigning responsibility for what was done to him. He imagined telling someone and protecting other children from being abused by this man. When I checked in with him, he said that he was really happy that he had protected other kids. This was something he had done in his imagination with bilateral stimulation. After another set of bilateral stimulation, he said, "I'm just right with the world. I feel right with the world. I felt with spirit and connected, and I felt in unison with my spirit—the spirit that I believe is greater than myself. I feel right with that." After he reported this, I asked him to go some more with that, really take it in, and then I added bilateral stimulation. After a few moments he opened his eyes and said, "I feel very protected by that spirit. Very protected. Very safe. Very loved."

I asked him again to go with that some more, and I continued bilateral stimulation. He was silent for a few minutes, then opened his eyes, crying: "I'm good. I'm a good guy. Such a good guy. I see myself. I'm so pure and I'm just feeling it, so much love for myself. I just feel so—I was never wrong, and I was never bad. I was just a good boy. Good, good boy. It's so nice to feel that."

After another round of bilateral stimulation, he opened his eyes and declared, "I like me, and I like hanging out with me. That's how much I like me. That's what it is, such a sweet and pleasant experience. You're the coolest dude. It's so cool. You're so cool. It's so fun to be with you. It's so nice."

I wiped tears from my eyes, deeply moved by all this love that was emanating from him, and then asked him if it was a good place to end. After he answered that it was, I asked him to check in with his body to see if there was anything left there that still needed to be cleared.

After taking a few moments to check inside, he reported that his body felt clear.

"It's warm and pulsating with goodness," he said. "It's alive all the way down to my toes."

Feeling deeply moved, we embraced. I felt touched by the love and openness that had infused both of us and the obviousness of his luminous True Self that was good and free of the contaminants of the abuse he had suffered as a child. It felt like grace and a blessing.

## Working with Blocks to Living from the True Self

Some people who have a spiritual practice and have done years of psychological work may still find that they are in some ways not living fully from their True Self. To facilitate working with these blocks, the therapist and client drop into a silent, resonant space and explore patterns of old beliefs, life-limiting constructs, energetic patterns, somatic symptoms—that which isn't True Self.

In my sessions, we begin by taking a moment to go inside to a quiet, still place, and then the client explores what they are experiencing. In this silent space, as the client explores their inner experience, I attune with their True Self and get a sense for the blocks they are describing. For example, if the client describes a pattern of not feeling like she is enough, I can direct her to find a time when she has felt like that recently, where she senses it in her body, and any beliefs that are associated with that. We can go in on it directly with bilateral stimulation to process it or by using what we call in AF-EMDR the bridging technique, tracing it back in time and exploring earlier roots to the pattern. I believe the key here is for the therapist to let go of any concepts and open their mind to possibilities. Inquiry without direction or interpretation allows for the discovery of what some of the impediments to True Self might be. I believe that when a therapist constrains their client with their views of them and interpretations of what their experience might mean, it closes the possibility of discovering what might be creating the block.

For example, a woman came to see me who was experiencing a strange sensation in her face and eyes that arose repeatedly during meditation. The sensation dissolved with mindful awareness, only to reappear each time she meditated. She had no idea what was causing this. We sat together in silence and brought up a memory of when this had occurred. In this case, there was no root that she could find, so we went in directly on the sensation in her face with bilateral stimulation. During the session she had a lot of sensation move through her face and body, and flashes of images of her mother began to appear. There was fear in her mother's eyes that she began to feel in her eyes and face. She remembered that her mother had lost a baby before she was born. She began to think that maybe the sensations that she was experiencing were not hers but belonged to her mother and her mother's fear of losing her too. After a few sessions focusing on these sensations, they disappeared. She realized that they never belonged to her, that they were her mother's fear that had been transferred into her nervous system. This did not originate in anything that had happened to her that was threatening. My capacity to hold the space and allow her to explore without interpretation what was arising allowed the fixation to dissolve and for her to experience a free flow of energy and wholeness in her body.

## Exploring Blocks to Living Fully

There are many possibilities that can create these blocks to True Self. Open exploration and inquiry are ways to begin to discover the causes. The more we clear old energies and patterns from our systems, the more we recognize our True Self and can notice when there is something impeding it.

### PRACTICE: EXPLORING BLOCKS TO LIVING FULLY

(The following practice can be done with bilateral stimulation, auditory stimulation, rattling, drumming, or any other form of bilateral stimulation—or without bilateral stimulation.)

Close your eyes and go inside. Take a deep breath, filling your belly, chest, and throat. Hold it a moment, then exhale slowly from your throat, your chest, and your belly. Relax; let go with the exhalation. Now take another breath. Take your breath in from deep in the earth, filling your belly, chest, and throat. Hold it a few moments. Now exhale, releasing from your throat . . . chest . . . and belly. Relax. Let go. Let yourself settle into the present moment.

When you feel yourself relax, ask yourself, *In what ways am I not living fully? What old patterns or beliefs keep me from expressing my full potential?* Take a moment and listen for what comes to you. It may come in words, pictures, or scenes. Write down what comes.

Where do these blocks originate from? Do they have roots in your history? Are they intergenerational or ancestral messages or patterns? Listen to what comes. Write it down.

Do these blocks come from something that happened to you in a past life? If the answer is yes, ask what happened. See what arises.

Are you carrying energies that don't belong to you? If yes, ask what they might be. Where do they come from?

After you have some answers, you can decide what you want to do to release the blocks. In some cases, just bringing awareness to the patterns helps to release them. For some of us, EMDR targeting the roots can help clear them and return us to our True Self. Intergenerational and past-life traumas can also be released with EMDR. In chapter 8 you learned several tools for energy clearing and developing energetic sovereignty.

## The Importance of Choosing a Therapist or Healer Who Can Resonate with Your True Self

Sitting with someone who attunes to your True Self facilitates your self-remembering. Like a tuning fork, you resonate with them resonating with you, and you both find yourselves recognizing the purity and unique expression of the True Self. In contrast, if your therapist or healer sees only your hurt places and does not recognize your True Self, you feel the constraint, and it can impede your healing process.

## PRACTICE: WORKING WITH THE TRUE SELF

Here's what it can look like to align with your True Self in a hypothetical situation.

Imagine you feel stuck in your life. You feel dissatisfied in many areas and want to find a way to move forward. You want a relationship but are not taking steps to find one. You want more satisfying employment and yet can't find a way to make changes. No matter what other people suggest, you find a way to negate it with reasons it won't work. All these examples seem like an underlying energetic pattern at play to all the stuckness. Since you have a meditation practice and are comfortable doing inner work, you can try the following.

Take a few moments to close your eyes and quiet your mind. If working with a therapist, it can be helpful if both the therapist and client do this so you both are centered before beginning the work. You can imagine going to your Peaceful Place, doing the grounding cord exercise, and calling your energy back to you.

After this, you want to connect with your True Self using the practice outlined earlier in this chapter. Ask yourself, *Can I connect with my True Self, the part of me that has always been there, the core of who I am beyond any conditioning? It may have existed even before this life. Can I get a sense of my True Self?*

If you have had an experience in the past in which you have connected with your True Self, you can bring this memory to mind.

If you can connect with the sense of your True Self, you can imagine the feeling expanding into more of your body and filling you up. You can use bilateral stimulation as you imagine doing this.

If the expansion doesn't feel right to do, skip it and move on to exploring any blocks to the expression of your True Self. Ask yourself, *As I connect with the sense of my True Self, what do I notice that may be blocking its expression? What is impeding the full expression of who I am?* This is where you can begin to inquire about body sensations, emotions, or beliefs that block expression.

Maybe you discover a blocked feeling in your heart. You can explore what this might be. Where did this originate from? Does it belong to you or to someone else? Are there beliefs connected with this sensation? Are there emotions? For example, you might report the emotions associated with the block in your heart to be fear and anxiety: *It isn't safe to express myself.* You can ask yourself, *Where did this come from?* Is it from your history, someone in your family, or even your ancestry? If you feel the belief is from your own history, and you can identify the source, it can be the focus of an EMDR session.

If you feel it is an old family prohibition, you can explore where it might have originated from. For example, if women in your lineage did not speak their minds or express themselves in any way, this may be the pattern you identify. This prohibition may have been passed down through the generations and was given to you, even though you are a modern woman and don't subscribe to the outdated conventions.

You can ask if there is an image that represents that prohibition from your family. You may have a picture that comes to mind that represents the entire lineage, such as an elder woman beating a younger woman for speaking her mind. This image can be targeted with EMDR. Compassionate, wise resource figures can also be brought to the women in the lineage to help heal and correct the pattern.

After identifying and addressing the blocks to True Self, you can return to the sense of your True Self and see if the work you have done helped. If there are still blocks, and you have time, you can continue to explore them and to clear them with the tools you have. If you identify other blocks, and you don't have time to address them in this session, you can make a point to return to the True Self in future sessions to continue the work.

## Summary

### *Connecting with and Living from Your True Self*

Spending time regularly connecting with your True Self as part of a practice can help you find your way back to your inner knowing and alignment with your sense of what is right for you. It can help to cultivate an inner compass that you can learn to trust and listen to. Nonjudgmental inquiry opens our minds to information that we don't understand but may be important for us to pay attention to. Over time, we become less concerned with the judgments of others and listen deeply and align with our inner sense of truth. In the next chapter you will see how one woman brought together many of the practices you have just learned in her own healing journey.

# 11

# Bringing Together Multidimensional Integrative Healing Practices

We've covered a range of multidimensional topics and practices over parts one, two, and three of the book so far, and I want to share an example of what it can look like when these separate elements come together in MDIH. This case story demonstrates the use of the techniques described in the previous chapters.

The client is a woman with early childhood abuse trauma who lost contact with herself and her energetic sovereignty during a visit with her family. In the session, we tapped in her Four Foundational Resources (Peaceful Place, Nurturing Figures, Protector Figures, and Wise Figures) and used the grounding cord. She called back her energy that had become dispersed, and I taught her how to create her energy bubble, to notice if there were any energies in her bubble that didn't belong to her, and to disinvite them. I guided her in connecting with her True Self and the natural world. All of these techniques helped her return to herself and establish her energetic sovereignty. She responded well to the methods and was able to successfully and enthusiastically use them on her own as part of a daily meditation practice.

As a note of caution: The case includes information that could be upsetting to some of you, as this client experienced childhood abuse.

## Disorientation and Loss of Self

A client I had not seen in many years, but with whom I had worked previously doing Attachment-Focused EMDR, contacted me with an urgent need to meet. She had recently returned home to be with her father, who was terminally ill. She thought when she arrived that he would not live long, but he revived and even improved during her visit. My client's history was traumatic and included abuse by her mother, father, and sister.

She had been fragmented and dissociated in the early days of our work but had integrated beautifully with the EMDR we did. It had been several years since she'd requested a session. We met virtually over Zoom for two hours. Because I knew her so well and we had a close, trusting relationship, we got to work immediately.

Returning to visit and stay in her parents' home with both of her parents and her sister was a nightmare for her. Her sister and mother were verbally abusive. There was so much abuse in her family that was never spoken of, and her mother and sister would do and say things they would later deny ever doing or saying. It was my sense that this denial was not purposeful; it was a manifestation of different or dissociated parts, and my client was the only one that remembered the interaction. She reported her sister screaming at her and saying horrible things to her and then later not having any recall of it. Her mother, too, told her she'd never wanted her, wished that she had never been born, and then did not recall saying that.

These painful and abusive contacts and the lack of recall on the part of her sister and mother was causing my client to lose her sense of reality. She was dissociating, losing her ground, her sense of self. She felt like she was going crazy. It seemed to me that she had entered the world of her childhood, where she had no power. It was important for her to have someone who knew her well outside of her family act as a sounding board to listen to her. Just that began to ground her.

During this session, she repeated something that was confusing to me—and significant. She kept saying that when her father died, she would no longer have a home. This perplexed me, as she did not live with her parents and in fact had been living in a beautiful place in a loving relationship for many years. I also was confused because I did not believe she had ever actually lived in the house where her parents currently resided. When I asked her these things, she was surprised and then told me that she had never lived in that house and that she did indeed love where she was living and her relationship with her partner was a good one.

By being asked and answering these simple questions, she quickly found some of her footing in the here and now. It seemed that home to her was the land, the area where her parents lived, not the house. Even if she was shut out of her parents' home, she would never be cut off from the land that she held to be sacred. This realization settled and grounded her. I told her that what I thought was going on was that she'd lost her center, her ground, her sense of self because she was lost in the energetic field of her family dysfunction.

This feeling of disorientation and loss of self was familiar to her. It was the same kind of dysfunctional, chaotic space that she grew up in. In that field of chaos, she lost her center and ground just as she had as a child. Even with our bad Zoom connection in which she looked fuzzy, the sound went in and out, and she froze from time to time, I could connect with her and help her remember her healthy, whole self.

## Restoring Boundaries

We had been through so much in the years of our work that our deep love bond and trust in each other was essential to the work we were able to do so quickly to help her restore her sense of wholeness. I told her that I thought that she had lost contact with herself and her energetic sovereignty. I had some ideas about how we might bring her back to herself and restore her boundaries. Here's what I did.

### The Four Foundational Resources

I called in and she tapped in her Four Foundational Resources. I asked her to imagine her Peaceful Place, and she tapped it in. She crossed her arms in front of her chest and tapped either shoulder bilaterally. It was a place nearby; she loved walking there on the land she loved. We then invited in her Nurturing Figures, Protector Figures, and Wise Figures and tapped them in one by one. Then she imagined them together as a team. Doing this made a difference for her, bringing her back to herself.

### Grounding Cord

Next, I guided her in the grounding cord. I directed her to close her eyes, go inside, and bring her attention to the base of her spine and allow the energy to pool there. "When you feel the energy there, imagine a cord made of anything you like. It can be a root, a shaft of light, a cord, anything, going deep into the earth. Imagine it going down into the dirt level and then deeper into the rock level, if it can go there. After the cord has gone down as far as it can go, imagine bringing the earth energy up through the cord. Let it come up through the channel in your back, bringing the earth energy. If it finds a place that is blocked, it can go around it and continue to bring the earth's energy up."

She closed her eyes and imagined doing this. I told her, "Notice how that feels. You can tap it in if you would like, or not."

After a few minutes of silence with her eyes closed and tapping, she stopped and reported what had happened. She told me she had a very powerful experience of the grounding cord on the land at her friend's house. She described the area as sacred land. The trees were special, and the land itself called her. She imagined a wide cord that was like a channel that went down into the earth and pulled up the energy from the land. She said it was very powerful.

### Energy Callback

After she did the grounding cord, we did an energy callback. I asked her to notice where her energy was. Was it scattered outside of herself? "Notice where your energy is. If it is extended way outside of yourself, you can call it back to yourself." I told her that sometimes I imagine hands helping to scoop it up and bringing it back to me. "Whatever works for you, call your energy back to yourself." She closed her eyes and imagined calling her energy back.

### Energy Bubble

After she signaled to me that she had accomplished the callback, I guided her in the energy bubble exercise. I asked her to notice where her energy bubble was. "There's a sphere of energy around you. Sometimes these bubbles get extended away from us. Can you notice where yours is?"

After a few minutes she opened her eyes and told me she was able to do this. I then wanted to assess if there was other people's energy in her bubble. I asked her to bring her awareness to her bubble and to see if anyone else's energy was in there. If it was, she could invite it to go where it needed to go outside of her bubble. She told me that she was able to do this too.

## True Self

Then we did the True Self exercise. I felt that part of her problem was that she had lost contact with her True Self. This is the Self that had been with her all her life. This is who she is without the conditioning and the effects of what happened to her in her life. I knew her True Self too, as it had been apparent in our work together in the years past. In retrospect, I think part of what was happening in the session was that I was aligning with her True Self. I was seeing, remembering, and resonating with it. I knew she could feel this, and it helped her return to herself. It is an attunement to the deeper Self that we both knew and remembered.

I asked her to go inside and connect to her True Self, "the part of you that's been with you your entire life. You might feel a glimmer of it or a spark." When she indicated that she'd located it, I asked her if she could imagine it growing and expanding. "Allow it to fill more of your body. Imagine it filling all your body, expanding into your cells, all the spaces." She said she could feel it. I told her she could tap either shoulder if she'd like. She closed her eyes and began to tap for several minutes. She told me she liked doing that. She said she felt much better.

## Nature Connection

At the end of the session, she told me she felt grounded and back to herself. She felt better able to cope with her family situation. I advised her to find time every day to do these practices in a place away from her family. I suggested maybe even sitting in her car if there wasn't any other place that was private. I also recommended that she walk in nature, get away from the house and the family chaos and connect to the natural world she loved so much.

In a message a few days later, she told me she was returning to her home after the visit with her family, that the meditation had been helpful, and she was grateful that she now felt she had a way to bring the spirit of the land with her. A couple of weeks later, she followed up again, letting me know she had begun to do the grounding cord, the energy callback, and all the other techniques I taught her on her own, four to five times a week, and that she felt that rooted sense growing even stronger.

## PRACTICE: UNITING THE PRACTICES OF MDIH

While there are many ways the practices of MDIH can be personalized and come together for unique experience and application, here is one example for you to try.

Close your eyes and go inside. Spend a few moments settling yourself. Feel yourself sitting; notice the contacts. Notice where your energy is. Is it extended out a distance from your body? Is it extended further in front of you or to the left or right side? Gently invite your energy to return to you. Gather it up; bring it back to you.

Now when you feel your energy returned to you, bring your awareness to the base of your spine. This is the place where your sit bones are. Invite energy to pool here at the triangle at the base of your spine. Now imagine a root or a cord, made of anything you wish, going down deep into the earth. Going down, down, down through the earth layer. Let it go down as far as it can go, maybe even as far as the rock layer. Take the time you need.

When you have gone as far down as you can, bring the earth energy back up through the cord, drawing it up through the channel in your back. It goes up, up, up into the base of your spine, and then it goes up the channel in your back. If you should sense that there is a block to the energy—a feeling or even an image that comes to mind—you can imagine the earth energy going around that blockage and continuing up the channel in your back. Continue bringing this earth energy up. It goes up from the base of your spine, into your lower back, then your middle back, into your neck and up into your head. Notice how that feels to have connected to the earth. You may want to add bilateral tapping to strengthen and integrate this feeling.

Now ask for a bubble of energy to surround you. It is transparent and in the shape of an egg. What are the boundaries of this bubble? Can you feel the edges of it? How far extended is it from you? You want the boundaries of the bubble to extend about one foot around your body, tending to extend further to the front and sides and closer to the back. To find it, you can start at the skin level and probe inch by inch until you have found where the edges are. If you find your bubble is misshapen or extended too far in front of you, you can call it back in closer to you.

See if there are any tears or openings in your bubble. If there are, imagine repairing them in whatever way feels good to you.

Now bring your awareness to the inside of your bubble. Are there energies inside that don't belong to you? They may have a color or form that is not yours.

If you discovered energy that isn't yours, you can inquire as to what it is and to whom it may belong. You can compassionately disinvite these energies and ask that they leave your bubble. You can imagine that they are leaving your bubble and going out into the universe where they need to go. You can call in a resource figure to help if you wish.

After you have created your energy bubble and invited any energies that are not yours to depart, call in your resources. Call in any resources you wish to be with you at this time. These are the resources that you feel would be most helpful and supportive to you.

These can include the resources you have tapped in, such as your resource figures: Nurturing Figures, Protector Figures, and Wise Figures. You can include spiritual figures, ancestral resources, and any other helpers that come to mind. As you imagine these figures, tap them in: right-left, right-left. Take the time you need to do this, imagining and evoking the feeling of each resource and then tapping it in. When you have completed this, imagine all of them together as a team supporting you, and then tap in the team.

Now allow yourself to connect to your True Self, your essential spiritual self. This essential part of yourself was there before you were born and has been there all your life. This is the part of you that has been with you through all you have experienced in your life yet has not been touched by any of it. This part of you is pure, good, innocent, wise, and resilient. It is the unique blueprint of your life expression. This is the core of your being. When you find a sense of it, or even a glimmer, invite the energy of your True Self to begin to expand. If it feels right for you, begin to tap right-left, right-left, and continue to do so as you invite your True Self energy to expand into all of the places in your body. It might begin in your heart and radiate out into your other organs, your limbs, all the cells of your body. Your True Self energy might have a color—notice that. Let it fill you. Notice, too, any places that feel blocked. As you invite your True Self energy to fill you, notice how this feels. Recognize this essential self, as it will help you to notice when you are not acting from this Self or if there is something that needs tending.

Remember, your True Self is always with you. You can contact it whenever you need to.

## Summary

### *Practicing the Techniques for Cultivating Energetic Sovereignty*

You have now seen how all the practices you have been introduced to in part three can come together. As my client discovered, when they are included in a daily meditation, you can cultivate more secure boundaries, the ability to return to your ground and True Self when off-balance, and increase nonjudgmental awareness when you discover you have absorbed undesirable energies into your bubble. All these practices, along with regular use of resources for support, help us feel more secure and have more control over what we allow into our energetic systems.

# PART FOUR

# Dimensions of Spirit Work

In part four we expand into further dimensions and describe ways to develop comfort and facility working with multiple dimensions through dreamwork and EMDR with after-death communications. Opening further to ways of working on multiple dimensions and building on skills developed in part three, you will learn how to recognize and assess spirit attachments and ways to facilitate their release.

12

# The Importance of Dreamwork in Multidimensional Integrative Healing

Dreamwork helps prepare us for Multidimensional Integrative Healing work in many ways. As we become more conscious in our dreams, we are able to more easily journey to the spirit world. For many, this can feel like crossing the veil, where one can receive communications from people who have crossed over, helping spirits, ancestors, angelic beings, and power animals. These dreams can also provide information to help guide us in life and serve as preparation for death. When we spend time recording our dreams and developing awareness during dreaming, our minds open and expand. We become comfortable with non-ordinary states of realty and our intuition increases. We develop an ability to listen openly with nonjudgmental awareness. All of these capacities serve to help us in our healing work.

I have remembered my dreams since I was a child, especially those that were vivid and compelling. Since my son's death, when I embarked on an intensified healing journey, my dreams have become more lucid and have often been spiritual. Some of the dreams have been teachings from ascended ancestors; others have been symbolic but evoked a feeling of awe. These dreams demanded I pay attention and write them down. Here is an example of one that created such great feeling I had to write it down and work with it so that I could more fully absorb its message.

> Dream: I am in a rural village in India. A middle-aged woman with long dark hair takes me by the hand and leads me up a dirt path that winds up a steep, rocky hill with bushes. She indicates that I should look around some bushes. I must grab hold of her as I lean over because I am afraid I will fall off the side of the hill. When I look over, I see appearing through the mist an enormous snow-covered mountain in the shape of a diamond. It seems very close. It is awesome, breathtaking.

The feeling of wonderment stayed with me all day. Afterward, I recognized it as being in the Himalayas and that this dream was a teaching I needed to pay attention to and uncover its message.

Later in meditation, I quieted my mind and then returned to the dream and accessed the feeling of awe it evoked. I began to rattle and ask for the meaning of the dream to come. I connected with the mountain and listened to what came to me.

The words *crystal mountain, diamond mountain* came. Clear white light emanated from it. When I asked its name, *Mount Meru* came. I recognized this as the sacred mountain also known as Mount Kailash. Revered by Tibetans, Hindus, and Jains, it is a multidimensional center of physical, metaphysical, and spiritual dimensions. As I sat with the energy of the mountain, I recognized the diamond light of clear mind. It illuminated the higher chakra at the crown of my head. I believed this was the quality I was being called to realize in this dream. This was the source of life, cosmic mother, clarity, freedom. Sitting with the feeling of the dream filled me with the clear light. This mountain is important to me. I have dreamed of it on several occasions, and each time I am filled with awe and clear light.

These dreams that have come since my son's death, bringing important teachings and realizations, have also opened me even more fully to multiple dimensions of reality. In the 1970s I was influenced by the writing of Carlos Castaneda and the teaching of Yaqui Juan Matus. In these books, which many now believe to be fiction, Castaneda emphasizes the importance of recalling dreams and working with them to develop the ability to dream lucidly. The psychophysiologist Stephen LaBerge, the author of *Lucid Dreaming: A Concise Guide to Awakening in Your Dreams in Your Life*, the spiritual teacher Andrew Holocek, the author of *Dreams of Light: The Profound Daytime Practice of Lucid Dreaming*, and others have written extensively about this practice. After my son died, I also began to meet him in the dream world. I believe my development of lucid dreaming helped open the portal to these meaningful, tender visits.

In January 2022, when I journeyed to the Ecuadorian Amazon and spent time with Sapara and Achuar shamans, I learned that dreamwork was an essential part of their spiritual practice. Community members come together to recount their dreams every morning as part of their ancestral spiritual tradition. This practice begins in childhood.

According to Manari Ushigua, the Sapara shaman and teacher, dreams help us connect to our intuition and interact with the spirit world as well as the world around us. Dreams provide vital information for what will happen the following day, weeks, and months. This information has helped prepare his people for events that would impact their lives. Through our dreams, we can receive information and instructions about our daily activities, work, family, friends, and more. Understanding these messages allows us to become our own spiritual guide and leader. Dreamwork is a means to connect to the wisdom of the earth and spirit world. Finally, dreamwork helps connect us to the Makihaunu, the Sapara word for the spirit world, where there is information to learn and future things to pay attention to now.

## My Dream Practice

I keep a journal by my bedside. Nights when I want to remember my dreams, I make a conscious intention to remember them. As I move toward a conscious waking state, I allow the dream to reveal itself so I can be with it and remember it. I don't have to understand what it means. I write down my dreams upon awakening. Later in meditation, I sit with the dream and bring it back up. I allow my mind to open and float in the dream state, providing space for it to unfold a bit to see if it will reveal more of what it wants to tell me. I have found that very compelling dreams seem to insist that I write them down. They remain in my awareness, nudging me as if they want to be remembered and understood.

Sometimes I add bilateral stimulation as I recall the dream, which can help to open up a free-associative process that allows the dream to reveal its message. I will describe how you might do that in the practice below.

## Dreamwork Practices Using Bilateral Stimulation Derived from EMDR

I found that with EMDR, people often had vivid dreams after sessions that I encouraged them to write down. When we used EMDR on these dreams, they brought deeper understanding and healing to the client, very often with insights and associations they never would have made with traditional analysis or using free-associative processing without bilateral stimulation. I have even used bilateral stimulation on dreams that felt to the client to be significant but not distressing, with the result that they connected to deeper meaning and layers of insights they found helpful.

Dreams make excellent focuses for EMDR processing because they are doorways into the unconscious and provide a wealth of material. Often clear and vivid dreams arise between EMDR sessions as a continuation of the work that was done in session.

There are different ways to work with dreams. When working with a significant dream, it is important to enter back into the dream state as much as possible. You can begin with a relaxed state, going to your Peaceful Place, calling in your resource figures, using the grounding cord, and calling back any energies that are dispersed. When you are in a settled state, bring up the dream. Open your senses and recall any imagery or a felt sense of the dream. When processing dreams, we want the dream to reveal itself. There can be many hidden layers of the dream.

I want to caution you that dreams can reveal information from the unconscious mind that is distressing. If you are concerned about what a dream may reveal, seek guidance from someone who can provide safety as you do this work. The following are two suggested practices for those who are prepared for what might be uncovered in the processing.

## PRACTICE: EXPLORING THE MOST COMPELLING PART OF A DREAM

Close your eyes and go inside. Take a deep breath, filling your belly, chest, and throat. Hold the breath a moment, then exhale slowly from your throat, your chest, and your belly. Relax; let go with the exhalation. Let yourself settle into the present moment. You might wish to go to your Peaceful Place and call in resource figures you wish to be with you as you enter the dream.

When you feel yourself relaxed, bring up the dream as vividly as possible. Scan the dream and identify the most compelling or emotionally significant part of the dream. What image represents the most significant part of the dream? Next, identify the emotions and body sensations that you notice. These should be readily available. Are there any immediate thoughts or beliefs that are associated with this scene? It can be helpful to write these things down if you are able to stay with the dream feeling.

When all of these elements are activated, begin bilateral stimulation. You can tap on the sides of your legs, cross your arms and tap either shoulder, or use any type of bilateral stimulation that you wish. As you tap, allow images, emotions, new memories, or any information to arise in awareness without censoring it. This is a kind of free-associative processing.

You might tap for a while. When important information arises, you can stop, write it down, then begin bilateral stimulation again for another round. If the information that is arising should link to any disturbing material, you can call in your resources for help or return to your Peaceful Place.

Every once in a while, return to the dream scene you began with to check it. If there is still information revealing itself, continue with bilateral stimulation.

Keep bilateral stimulation going with check-ins with the original scene until the dream seems like there is no longer information to be processed or revealed. When it feels complete, ask for the meaning of the dream, the message, or what you have learned or understood from the dream process. It could be something like *I'm strong and capable* or *I am safe now*. After receiving this information, add bilateral stimulation to link it to the dream scene.

## PRACTICE: PROCESSING A DREAM WITH MANY PARTS

Some dreams have many different parts. Note them as you recount the dream. You can break the dream into the different parts, starting with the beginning of the dream. After completing the processing of that part, move on and check in on the next part. If charged, you can process that part. Continue processing each part to completion until the entire dream has been processed and has revealed to you some understanding or meaning.

Close your eyes and go inside. Spend a few moments settling your mind in whatever way works for you. You might wish to go to your Peaceful Place and call in any resource figures you wish to be with you as you enter the dream.

When you feel yourself relaxed, bring up the dream as vividly as possible. If it has many parts, recall those too. If you can, write these down.

What is the first image in the dream that feels significant to you? As you recall it, notice what emotions you are feeling, what you notice in your body, and any thoughts or beliefs that immediately come up. Then begin bilateral stimulation, allowing for the free-associative processing of the dream.

The dream may unfold like a lucid dream, remaining in symbolic form. It may immediately link to a memory, or go in and out of memory and dream symbolism.

From time to time, go back and check the beginning of the dream to see if it has changed and if there is more to process. If there is no longer information there to process, and the emotional charge has reduced or disappeared, scan the rest of the dream and see if there are other places that feel significant.

If you find another dream scene that feels important, focus on that with bilateral stimulation in the same way you did with the first scene.

Continue in this way through all the significant scenes, allowing each one to reveal its message. When you get to the end of all the scenes, scan the entire dream from beginning to end, looking for any places that still have emotional valence. When you discover one, add bilateral stimulation to it to allow it to clear. This can happen very quickly. Continue focusing awareness on any places that have charge and using bilateral stimulation until you can no longer find any.

When you feel the dream has revealed to you all the information, ask yourself for the meaning or understanding that goes with the dream. When you have those words, add bilateral stimulation to help link them to the dream itself.

Sometimes each segment of the dream has a different meaning to it. You might want to ask for what that is and then link it with that segment. At the end of the session, when all the dream segments have been processed and the meaning linked, you can ask if there is a meaning for the entire dream. If there is, you can link that meaning or understanding as you review the entire dream sequence.

For many people, the dream immediately links to a memory. This memory then becomes what you focus the processing on and the scene you refer back to during the processing. At the end of the session, you link the meaning or understanding that fits with the memory and then check the dream, if time allows. If it seems useful, link the meaning or understanding that goes with the dream.

## Summary

### *Dreamwork as a Spiritual Practice*

Dreamwork is an important contribution to MDIH. Recalling our dreams, recording them, and working with them provides information that is helpful in healing and advancing spiritual development. Familiarity and comfort with dream states teach us ways to venture into other dimensions and receive information that can guide our lives.

# 13

# EMDR and After-Death Communication

During EMDR, many people have after-death communications when processing the death of someone. The psychologist Allan Botkin, who worked for many years at North Chicago Veterans Affairs Center, has researched and documented these experiences and written about them in his book *Induced After Death Communication*. Though I don't set out to purposely induce these communications, they have arisen spontaneously during EMDR sessions when the focus has been the processing of grief and loss. My goal in therapy is always the alleviation of my client's suffering, not the induction of a kind of experience. For that reason, in this chapter I describe some of the after-death communications clients have spontaneously experienced during EMDR processing of grief and loss but not practices for inducing these experiences.

After-death communications feel sacred and authentic to clients, who are often surprised and moved to tears. I have come to almost expect them when there has been a loss that still feels raw and distressing. The deceased can be someone clients are close to, such as a family member; someone with whom they have unfinished business; or someone they have harmed in some way.

In working to help clients heal from grief that is impacting their life, I first use EMDR to process any traumas related to the death. Dr. Botkin also suggests this approach. The traumas often impede the connection with the deceased. After the processing, if the client expresses that there is still regret or there was something incomplete in the relationship when the person died, I invite the client to say or do anything they wish they could have done at the time: "Is there something you would like to say to your mother that you weren't able to say at the time?" If they say yes, I say, "Imagine that" and add bilateral stimulation. I also suggest that if it feels right to them, they should stay open to a response from the deceased: "If it feels right to you, stay open to a response from your mother." As they imagine these things, we add bilateral stimulation. It is during this time that after-death communications arise. These communications can come in the form of words, symbols, or just a sense of a message. Over the years working with individual clients, supervising practice sessions during EMDR trainings, and consulting to EMDR clinicians, I have observed or worked with hundreds of these cases.

## Communication for the Heartbreaking Grief of Siblings Loss

The first time this occurred, I was working with a woman who was grieving the death of her elder brother, who had died suddenly and unexpectedly. She was struggling with depression, and she had no spiritual beliefs or sense of life after death to provide comfort. She had lost her faith when she was a young girl, when her baby sister died. Nothing anyone could tell her brought her any comfort. How could a loving God do this?

In the middle of an EMDR session focusing on the loss of her brother, she suddenly gasped. She had seen an image of three numbered doors, and the middle door opened to show her brother holding her baby sister in his arms. They were glowing with the most radiant light she had ever seen. They were smiling with love in their eyes directed at her. She was shocked and frightened by this very vivid scene. She could hear and see them, and she felt they were there with her. Because this experience was far from anything she had ever experienced before, she asked to stop the EMDR immediately. "What does this mean?" she demanded, her eyes wide in wonderment.

"What does it mean to you?" I asked. "What are they communicating to you?"

"We are happy, and we want you to be happy too," her brother told her. As she related these words, she began to cry. She told me that they communicated to her that they were together someplace and that they wanted her to get on with her life. She again asked me what this meant, and I suggested that she honor the experience and see how it affected her.

When I saw her the following week, she told me that now when she thought of her siblings, she felt a deep sense of peace rather than heartbreaking grief. She said that she knew that they were okay and not alone. She now believed that death was not the end of life but a transition. "I know that they are alive and happy somewhere together. And when I die, I will see them again." She said she felt tranquility and spirituality she had not experienced before. This experience changed her life.

Years later, she continued to be at peace with the losses, and she regained happy memories of her siblings that she had lost after their tragic deaths. She missed them but was no longer troubled with grief around the holidays or special occasions. This experience also inspired an opening to spirituality and exploration.

## Healing Communication After a Death by Suicide

In another case of after-death communication, a woman in my EMDR basic training at Omega Institute volunteered to do a demonstration with me in front of the class. She wanted to work on the trauma she lived with since the passing of her ex-boyfriend when she was in college. Though they had broken up before he died by suicide, she felt that she had not treated him well in the end and that she was responsible for his death. She was haunted by the image she had created in her mind as to what his last moments had been like. This session was powerful and very moving.

I asked her to think of the worst part of the story. She reported that it was the horrible picture she had created in her mind of what her ex-boyfriend had experienced in his final moments. In order to activate the network where the trauma was stored so that we could begin the EMDR processing of the event, I asked her for the most disturbing part of the memory. She described a scene that she had created in her mind of his last moments. I asked her what emotions she felt, what she experienced in her body, and what belief she held about herself. She said she felt terrible guilt; she was sick in her stomach and believed that she was responsible. With all of this activated, I started bilateral stimulation—in her case, she had asked me to tap rhythmically on her knees. I instructed her to "let whatever happens happen without censoring it," and she began to rapidly process the trauma.

Shortly after the tapping started, she went into what she described as an altered state of consciousness. I gently guided her by asking what was happening between the sets of tapping. She was in touch with the guilt that she felt, not so much for his death but for some of the unkind things that she had said and done during their disagreements the year prior to his death.

She cried as she told him she was sorry she had hurt him and asked for his forgiveness. She shared that he suddenly appeared before her as a beautiful radiant angel in the sky and told her that he had forgiven her for whatever there was to forgive. He said whatever she had done to hurt him was a small part of their relationship and that her love and kindness were what he took with him and held on to. He shared that he was okay and she didn't have to worry. "You have suffered long enough," he said, "and I don't want you to suffer anymore." A huge sense of relief and peacefulness overcame her. By the end of our session, her level of distress was very much diminished, but she still felt triggered at the thought of how he had died.

I asked her to go inside and picture the image once more, and I started to tap bilaterally on her knees again. She told me she felt like a circuit board in her head started to turn on and colored lights started flashing furiously. Then she saw a split-scene image in her mind with him as the angel on one side and the scene of his passing on the other. The angel swooped down across the divided screen into the scene of his passing and said, "This is not me anymore. I left this form many years ago." The scene transformed into a stairway leading up into the starlit heavens. As he walked up the stairs, he said, "I'm sorry that my death caused you so much pain, but please understand I am no longer in pain. Forgive me." In that moment she was finally able to comprehend that she truly was not responsible for his death and was finally free from the pervasive guilt.

## Communication for Resolution of a Tragic Accident

Momi, whom I describe in my book *Transforming Trauma: EMDR*, came to see me for fear of flying. During EMDR processing of an imagined flight, she made a link that her anxiety was associated with the sudden death of her best friend in a plane crash when they were both young women. Her friend—a young mother—was killed when her small plane got caught in a storm and crashed into a mountain. Momi had always believed that her friend's death was untimely and tragic. As she processed with EMDR how she imagined her friend had died, she suddenly began to receive what she felt was direct communication from her friend. Her friend told her that it wasn't the dying that was the problem; it was the fear leading up to the big bang. After the big bang, there was peace. She also told her that from her after-death perspective, which provided a vast view of time and space, it had been her time to go and that everything was as it should be. There was no problem. This communication freed Momi from the sense of tragedy. During our session, she began to spontaneously imagine her own death in a plane crash with what she called "the big bang." As she did this with bilateral stimulation, she reported feeling peace. A fanciful song and dance came to her on an imagined flight, with the words *Could go, probably won't.* She saw herself singing the song and dancing down the aisle of the plane. At the end of the session, she reported finding peace in the truth of her relative safety and knowing that physical death was not the end of life.

## Key Points on After-Death Communications

Some key points regarding after-death communications for EMDR therapists:

- These can occur spontaneously during EMDR processing of a death.
- These can be surprising, even shocking, for the client. Be reassured that this has been reported frequently by others.
- For therapists, it is important to stay open and do not interpret the meaning of these experiences. Ask the client what these experiences mean to them.

- When there is unfinished business with a person who has died and the client is processing regret, ask them if there is something that they would like to say that they did not say at the time. If they say yes, guide them to go with that, and then add bilateral stimulation. You can suggest that they stay open to a response from the deceased. A communication may be received in words, symbols, or an immediate knowing.

- You can ask clients who have lost a loved one if they have had dreams or received signs from the loved one. For example, a friend of mine who died was very connected to dragons. The two weeks after her death I encountered multiple unexpected experiences with dragon symbols: A consultee of mine came to session wearing a dragonfly pendant and told me she felt she had to wear it that day. A waiter in a Japanese restaurant who did not know me or my friend randomly told me I was having dragon roll for lunch that day. Later, that same week at a market in a local park, I found a dragonfly tapestry displayed that I had never seen before. I have found that often these experiences occur with frequency in the weeks following the death and then taper off and stop. These kinds of experiences can be linked in with bilateral stimulation as the client recounts them so that they are integrated more fully into their understanding, and they receive the communication from the other side.

- Remember that these experiences are sacred. Together you enter a liminal space that can transform your lives and move you deeply.

Over the years in my personal and professional life, I have learned that those whose physical bodies have died often try to communicate with their friends and family following their physical death. I believe it is important for the dead and the living to pay attention to these communications—to listen to them, receive them, and respond if necessary. Often people are frightened by hearing from the dead and shut them out. In my experience, these communications tend to happen the first weeks after the death and then taper off or cease. The completion of the communication can be healing for the deceased and the bereft loved one.

### PRACTICE: SOME RECOMMENDATIONS FOR RECEIVING AFTER-DEATH COMMUNICATION

Pay attention to your dreams, especially in the first days and weeks after a death. Loved ones often attempt communication through dreams. Communication can come through seeing them in a dream scene, through symbols, or even hearing their voice.

Before going to sleep at night, you can ask for a visit from your loved one. It can help if you already have a dream practice or are adept at remembering your dreams. These visits can occur in a kind of liminal space between sleep and waking. These are a kind of lucid dream. If your loved one appears in a dream and you are conscious at the time, you can have a visit and conversation with them. I have had many of these with my son, who always appears healthy and his best self.

Look for signs or symbols that are associated with the deceased. My friend loved dragons and dragonflies, and these symbols showed up frequently in different ways the first weeks following her death.

Friends and family of the deceased may have had communications from them. Share information. After my son's death, his former girlfriend began to "channel" him with lots of information he wanted shared with his friends and family.

If a loved one shows up in a dream or vision and seems to want to communicate with you, stay open to receiving it. Did they leave unfinished business? Do they want to say goodbye or tell you that they love you? If you can, communicate back to them through your thoughts. Don't be afraid and shut them out. By allowing the completion of the communication, you are helping to free them to cross over.

## Summary

### *Opening to the Possibility of After-Death Communication with EMDR*

In this chapter you were introduced to how EMDR often induces after-death communications when processing grief and loss and how this can be profoundly healing. EMDR seems to lift the veil between dimensions and opens the pathway to connecting the deceased with the living. You also learned recommendations for receiving after-death communication so that you can continue connecting with those who have crossed over.

# 14

# Recognizing and Assessing Spirit Attachments

There are times when we experience symptoms or problems that are difficult to explain, especially if we are constrained to approach them through a Western psychology lens. We may see people not physically present or hear voices. We may be frightened by these experiences that may appear "psychotic," yet we have no other symptoms that support that diagnosis. Perhaps we feel the presence of an energy that feels foreign to us, or we have nightmares or flashbacks of events that are not from this lifetime. I have heard these reports all my career as a therapist, as well as from friends and colleagues. Because I have been open to multiple dimensions of reality, I have recognized that, in some cases, these things may be indications of spirit attachments.

Spirit, soul, or energetic attachments occur when a person whose body has died attaches to a person with a body. The person whose physical body has died may have died recently or a long time ago. The person could be a family member, an ancestor, or someone we have no relationship to at all. They may attach to someone they have an affinity with or someone they feel can help them in some way. These souls often have incomplete lives and seek to complete something before they can cross over. Often they do not know that their body has died. This chapter provides information about how to recognize and assess these attachments. In the next chapter I provide ways to work with them compassionately using inquiry and resources to release them.

I have been learning to recognize and work with spirit attachments and am not by any means an expert in working with this phenomenon. What I wish to impart here is what I have learned from my mentor and spirit worker Jean Schneider and a group of psychotherapist colleagues. We have been learning from Jean and sharing our experiences from our personal work with her, our psychotherapy work with clients, and during Multidimensional Integrative Healing retreats I have been offering. I feel that it is important for us to understand how to recognize this phenomenon and know a little about how we can help the spirit that has become attached.

Many spiritual and religious traditions recognize that physical death is not the end of life. Many also recognize that, for various reasons, spirits from people whose bodies have died may not always cross over and may become attached to living people. Since teaching, traveling, and studying in countries outside of the United States and Europe, I have been introduced to other ways of viewing life, death, and the normalization of spirit attachments. These things are not part of how we in the West view the world or are even allowed to talk about it. However, whether we believe in these things or not, our clients report these experiences and are often troubled by them. In my experience, if we don't have a concept for something, it is as if it doesn't exist or lacks validity. Because of this, when people experience symptoms that indicate spirit attachments, they are pathologized, misdiagnosed, mistreated, and even medicated for something that could be recognized and worked with successfully by a person who understands how to work with it.

An example of this was a case of an Iraqi war veteran whose therapist I was providing consultation to. This man was haunted by a child who kept appearing to him, like a visual hallucination, and would not leave. His psychiatrist diagnosed him as psychotic and recommended antipsychotic medication, even though he had no other symptoms that would point to that diagnosis. When I heard about this case, I told the therapist that I didn't believe that her client was psychotic; rather, for some reason, the spirit of the child was attempting to communicate something to the man that she needed to resolve. I suggested that the therapist ask the veteran to ask the child what she wanted to tell him and allow the completion of the communication. The therapist followed my recommendation, and the man allowed the child to tell him what she needed to say. After this was done, the child left and the "haunting" ceased. No antipsychotic medications were necessary. If this man had been medicated for psychosis, the medication may have masked his symptoms, and he would have suffered from the side effects without freeing him from the underlying cause.

## Recognizing Spirit or Soul Attachments

Spirit attachments can present in several ways. You may experience physical sensations or problems that seem to arise out of nowhere and lack explanation. One woman who has learned to recognize for herself when energies have attached to her said that when attachments have occurred, she has a ringing in her ears, she feels nauseous, becomes bloated, gains weight, feels like she is not in her body, and feels floaty and dissociated. When these symptoms appear, she knows that she needs to get help to release the beings who have attached to her.

Some people experience an unexplained feeling or emotional state. When explored, they say that what they are experiencing does not feel that it belongs to them. Another possible sign of spirit attachments is feeling blocked in some way. When exploring the block, it seems linked to someone or something that has become energetically attached.

Many people with spirit attachments describe feeling disconnected from themselves and have difficulty connecting to their True Self. They may have problems doing the grounding cord or True Self exercise. They cannot regain their energetic sovereignty. Some people, like the example of the veteran, hear a voice or see things or people yet have no other psychotic symptoms. Others report feeling as though they are carrying something that does not belong to them. They may describe having an emotional reaction to something that is out of proportion to the situation, or that they feel or sense something in their energy bubble or body that isn't theirs.

Another example of spirit attachment occurred during a guided meditation to work on ancestral cords that I led in a Multidimensional Integrative Healing retreat. Evelyn tearfully reported that she had something attached to her lower abdomen. She said it was a dark energy that felt female. I asked Evelyn if the energy belonged to her. "No, it didn't," she responded. Because I sensed that this might be a spirit attachment, I began then to address it directly through Evelyn. I told her (the spirit) that we were there to help her in any way that we could. I asked her a series of questions that Evelyn responded to, speaking for the spirit. She told me that she was a human female. I compassionately informed her that her body had died and that she was in spirit form. This was a shock to the spirit, and she needed space to accept and process this, as it was upsetting to her. She began to cry. I told her that though her body had died, she still had life but was no longer in a body.

Because spirits often attach to someone because they need help, I asked the spirit what she needed. Through Evelyn she communicated that she had been a woman who had died during the Japanese occupation of the Philippines, and she was related to Evelyn. She had lost something that belonged to her that was from her lower abdomen. I wondered if it was her womb. I asked if she had lost a child, and she indicated yes. She had been a "comfort woman," a woman enslaved by the Japanese soldiers for sex. She indicated she had been violated by many soldiers and very traumatized.

I again asked her what she needed. She said she needed to tell Evelyn that she could enjoy sex. It was okay now. She also needed to be heard and for Evelyn to know what had happened to her. The woman communicated to Evelyn what had happened to her, including that a baby had been taken from her.

After this was shared, I wondered if she was ready to cross over and release her attachment to Evelyn. I asked her what her beliefs were about where a person went when they died. Evelyn whispered, "Heaven." I then asked what she needed to cross over. She responded that she wanted her family and to go home.

Evelyn described to us what happened next.

"Her mother appeared at that time. She took her by the hand, and they traveled to a mountainous area that was green with palm trees." Evelyn believed that this was where she had come from and where her people had hidden from the Japanese invaders. She said the woman's mother took her on a path through the mountains and then they were out of sight. She had crossed over.

When we checked in, Evelyn said she felt that the woman's spirit had detached from the cord in her abdomen. She was tearful and emotional through the entire process. She felt that this was a woman related to her. Puzzled by what had been communicated, she had never heard that someone from her family had been captured and enslaved during the war. Prior to this experience, she had believed that everyone had escaped into the mountains and had been safe from the Japanese soldiers.

The next day when we checked in, she told me she felt a space in her abdomen where the soul had attached. I asked if she wanted to fill it with her True Self light or anything else. She said yes; she thought that would help. She closed her eyes and imagined blue light from her ancestral sacred well filling it, and then light came from the earth filling the empty space. Visibly moved by this experience, with tears in her eyes she said she felt this was healing for her. She said upon reflection that the ancestral spirit had needed help and had attached to her to get that from her and the retreat group.

## Perpetrator Energies

While the previous story demonstrates support needed for those who were harmed, it's important to be aware that there are also times when the identified energies belong to people who have caused harm. These dark energies or even soul parts have become attached. For example, you might identify it as feeling like the energy of a family member that you've been carrying in your system your whole life.

An example of this was described by a client of mine during an EMDR session focused on abuse by a group of men. She described her young self as leaving her body and "merging with the perpetrator energy." She was able to recognize that those energies belonged to her abusers and not to her. The energy of the abusers had attached to her and were released in our EMDR session.

If you sense an energy that feels foreign and unwelcome, you can ask the energy why it is with you. What does it need? These energies can also be released by discovering ways to help release them. Calling in resource figures to assist in this release, bringing in healing light from a divine source, or even composting them into the earth can be helpful.

## PRACTICE: ASSESSING THE SIGNS AND USING INQUIRY TO DETERMINE WHAT HAS ATTACHED

Signs that may indicate spirit attachments include:

- Physical sensations or problems that are unexplained
- An unexplained feeling or emotional state
- Feelings of being blocked in some way
- Feeling disconnected from yourself
- Problems connecting to your True Self
- Hearing a voice in your head that doesn't belong to you, with no other psychotic symptoms or hallucinations
- A feeling like you are carrying something that does not belong to you
- Trouble sleeping
- Disturbed dreams

After exploring the possibility of spirit attachments by considering the common signs of attachment, gather information about what has attached by asking a series of questions—to yourself, if you are doing this for yourself, or to your client if you are a healer working with someone. In some cases, direct the questions to the spirit.

You can ask questions like the following:

- Does this energy have a shape?
- Does it have a color?
- Does it feel like it belongs to you?
- If it doesn't belong to you, does it belong to someone else?

If the answer comes that feels like it belongs to someone else, you can begin to direct questions to the energy or spirit.

Let's imagine a situation in which you feel a strange energy on your left side. Upon examination, you describe it as cloudy, sad, and like it doesn't belong to you. The feeling came on suddenly, seemingly out of the blue. You begin to explore this with inquiry. You notice that it feels like human energy. It feels like it is from someone who no longer has a body.

If you identify that it is an energy from a person who has died, you can ask if it is male or female, man or woman, baby or child. You can ask if the energy knows that its body has died. The inquiry you do depends on the answers you get. If you determine that the energy is a human that no longer has a body, you now in essence will be working with the being that has attached to you and needs help.

## PRACTICE: ASSESSING FOR SPIRIT ATTACHMENTS USING CLEAR AND OPEN SPACE METHOD

Another way to determine if you have a spirit attachment is to use a method that contrasts a clear and open space feeling with what you might be sensing attached to you.

Close your eyes and go inside. Spend a few moments settling your mind in whatever way works for you. You might wish to call your energy back to you, do the grounding cord, go to your Peaceful Place, and call in any resource figures you wish to be with you.

When you feel yourself settled and present, imagine clear and open space. Some people can quickly imagine this; others may need prompts. Clear and open space might be the cloudless night sky, the vast ocean, the desert, or a high place with an unobstructed view. These things can evoke that feeling.

After calling up what you identify as clear and open space, notice what that feels like. When you have a felt sense of the clear and open space, bring your attention to the space in front of you. Does it feel the same or different? If it feels different from the clear and open space, how so? How does it feel different? Does it feel heavy? Is there a color, shape, or texture associated with that? Is there an emotion? You want to write down what you notice.

You then move to the right side and repeat the inquiry, then to the left, and then to the back. You can even assess below and above, including all sides if you have time. You may discover that you have identified something present on more than one side of yourself. Notice what is affecting you the most.

For example, you have identified a heavy, dark energy on the front side of your body, and that feels the most significant to you. That is where you will begin. Often when we begin and release the strongest part first, it also releases the others without having to address them individually.

After identifying the place where you are going to work and the description of the energy there, you begin inquiry. This process is very much like I described earlier. You begin by asking if it is yours or not yours. For example, "Does this dark, heavy energy on your right side feel like it's yours or not yours?" If it's not yours, ask questions such as "Whose is this? Why are they there? Do they know that they don't have a body? Is there a purpose to this? What does it need?" Inquire with the assumption that everything has a place, everyone belongs somewhere, and every energy belongs somewhere.

The following are some of the questions to ask yourself when contrasting with clear and open space.

- Does this feel like yours or not yours?
- If not yours, ask more questions: Whom does it belong to? Is it someone you know? Is it a family member, ancestor, or someone from another time?
- Does this belong with a human?
- Was this ever a human?
- Is it masculine or feminine? Male or female?
- Is it a man, woman, girl, boy, or baby?
- Is there a reason this energy of . . . is with you?
- Do you have a body that is alive, or did something happen to your body? (Inquiry is directed at the energy.) Listen to the answer.

## Sensitivity to Attracting Energetic Attachments

It seems that some people are more vulnerable to attracting energetic attachments than others. There may be an ancestral connection to the being or a situational one (the person who died was in the same vicinity as the person whom they attached to), or that being came through someone else to you. It seems that some people are more psychically open to these attachments than others. As we do in EMDR, you want to ask them what they need. They may need to find their loved ones or know what happened to the others in the accident. They also might want to bring in resource figures of some kind, such as spiritual resources.

Beings may be attracted to someone they believe can help them. This may be what happened to the group of us at Esalen Institute when I led a group of women in a weekend retreat in Multidimensional Integrative Healing and EMDR. I'll share more about this story in the next chapter.

## Summary

### *Recognizing and Assessing Spirit Attachments*

In this chapter you learned ways to recognize spirt attachments and examples of what they can look like. You have also learned why some of us are more likely to attract them. Now that you have learned about how to recognize and assess spirit attachments, in the next chapter you will learn about how to release these attachments and help with their transition. This is sacred work that requires an open mind and a compassionate heart.

# 15

# Acknowledgment and Ritual to Facilitate Spirit Release

After you have recognized that there is a spirit or soul attached that used to have a body, and you have compassionately informed the spirit that its body has died, you can begin the process of facilitating the release. What follows are ways to facilitate spirit release and examples of this sacred work.

## Discovering What a Spirit Needs

The assumption in Multidimensional Integrative Healing is that every energy and being belongs somewhere. Our job is to help in any way we can to understand and help these beings or energies go where they need to go. When we direct our communication to the spirit that has attached, we can tell them, "I'm here to listen and help if I can. I'm not here to make you do anything. We will work with you to see what you need." The approach is of compassion, wonder, and curiosity, which opens awareness.

For those who are familiar with ego-state or parts work, the inquiry we do when working with spirit attachments is similar, except the goal is not to integrate the parts but to get to know them and their needs and to release them. The inquiry is directed at the spirit. You listen to what you feel is coming through as an answer. In my experience, the answers to the questions just come to me, and I respond. I also get pictures in my mind that arise spontaneously that provide information. Communication is initially aimed at reminding the spirit attachment that it has died and that it is not in its own body. After that, you want to find out what is needed for it to release and return to the spirit realms. Often this can be as simple as completing a communication, enacting a death ritual, or being reunited with a loved one from the attachment's life.

You can inquire about how they died: What happened? Sometimes images come to your mind and you answer from the perspective of the being. For example, the being might say that they were in a car accident that happened on an icy road at night. They didn't realize that they had died.

It can be shocking for the being to realize that they no longer have a body to return to. You might tell them, "We are so sorry that your body died." You want to create space for the sadness and recognition of the death of the physical body: "Do you remember what happened?" You can ask what they look like and how they are dressed. You might ask, "Do you know what year it was when your physical body died?" Listen to what they say. They may have died recently or many years ago. It might not even be in the country you are living in. What I have learned is that time and space are very different in other dimensions. A person could have been killed hundreds of years ago in a country on the other side of the world and has attached to you for some reason.

I have learned that a sudden death can prevent a person from crossing over. I knew because of the sudden and violent way in which my son was killed that he needed help. Though his spirit was visiting family and friends after his death, and those communications were ecstatic and joyful, I still worried that he was not okay and that some part of him had not crossed over. I was also concerned about the dark energy that surrounded his death and wanted that cleared from him and the rest of my family. I sent word out to my friends and found Jean Schneider, who was able to help in all these ways. Jean worked over several days, diligently using advanced skills to help my son cross over. After her work, I felt a shift, as did other members of my family. Prior to her work, my dreams were of trying to help him and searching for pieces of a puzzle that needed to be assembled. After her work, these dreams ceased, and I slept more peacefully.

Many people do not cross over if they are not provided the death rites of their people or tradition. For Native peoples who were forced to convert to Christianity and abandon their traditions, Christian burial rites may have prevented them from crossing over. When we discover that there is a soul or being that has not crossed over, we ask them what they need. What is keeping them here? We listen to what they say. Many need the burial rites of their religion or spiritual tradition to be performed. Who can perform that for them? What would it look like? We ask them to imagine everything they need. They may wish to imagine returning to their ancestral land, for chanting or prayers to be recited. They may wish to imagine their bodies prepared according to custom. There may be foods that they wish to be served.

For example, I had an experience of a dark, distressing energy attached to my right side that was causing me to feel disconnected from myself. After determining that it was a being that had died hundreds of years ago and had not crossed over, I began inquiry.

This being had died suddenly and didn't know he had died. When I asked him what he needed to cross over, he said that he needed to be remembered and his life honored. When I asked how he might do that, an image of a plaque with his name engraved on it appeared, and then an olive grove planted in his memory and those of his friends and family who had died. After I saw him receiving all of these things, I asked if he was ready to cross over. He called in a spiritual figure from his tradition to help him go up to heaven. A portal opened up, and I "saw" him being received on the other side. After these images, I felt a relief from the darkness on my right side and felt reconnected to myself again.

Some people do not cross over because they have unfinished business with the living. They have unresolved lives that need closure. In helping them, we can ask what they need to complete. When you discover what they need, you can suggest that they imagine what they need. It is a trial-and-error kind of process where you offer something they accept or reject, and then you try something else. Little by little, together you find what is needed. They then imagine doing these things. They may also wish to bring in resources to help them. You can use bilateral tapping, drumming, or rattling if that helps with this process.

I was working with a woman who felt unexplained guilt all of her life that she felt connected to a past life. After inquiry, she discovered that there was the spirit of a soldier who had died hundreds of years ago attached to her. This spirit did not know that he had died and no longer had a body. He felt guilty for abandoning his men. When I explained to him that he had died and no longer had a body and therefore had not abandoned his men, he was relieved. The communication of this information was the key that then allowed this spirit to be released and begin to cross over.

Does the spirit have a belief about what happens to their soul after the body dies? You can ask the being, "Help us understand your cosmology." If they don't know, give them options, such as going to heaven, into the earth, up, down, into the north or the west.

After they have imagined what they need to cross over and where they want to go, you can ask them if they are ready and if there is anything they need. They may want to invite a psychopomp being to accompany them. Psychopomps are guides who escort souls or spirits to the afterlife. The term originates from the Greek words *pompos* (conductor or guide) and *psyche* (breath, life, soul, or mind). Accounts of psychopomps exist worldwide through mythology, religion, sacred narratives, and people's experiences, including from near-death reports. Some of the most well-known psychopomps include the Greek god Hermes, the Egyptian jackal-headed god Anubis, the archangel Michael, and the female Valkyries of Norse mythology. Animals, birds—including crows, vultures, and owls—angels, and other beings have been identified as psychopomps. Ancestors, friends, and family members may also appear at the time of death and assist with the passage. This was the case for Dr. Eben Alexander, who had a near-death experience that he details in his book *Proof of Heaven*. While he was in a medically induced coma, a beautiful young woman accompanied him to the other side and in his journey before he returned to his physical body. He later discovered that this compassionate guide was a biological sister who had died many years before and whom he had never met.

When the being has completed what they need to do to cross over, and they indicate they are ready for their passage, you can ask them if they would like to invite someone or something to help them on their journey. You can offer possibilities from their spiritual, religious, or ancestral tradition. See what comes for them. You can invite a portal or an opening to be made for the passage and then invite them to go where they wish to go. In my limited experience with this, sometimes this has happened very quickly, even without a psychopomp being, when they complete what they need to complete. Whereas other times, they need more direction and help.

After the being or energy has been released, check in with yourself. How are you feeling? Some people may feel disoriented, as they have carried this energy with them for a long time and their system needs time to readjust. For those who have had physical symptoms or ailments caused by the attachment, they may experience a reduction or total alleviation. Some people may wish to imagine healing light of some kind filling in the space from what has departed. You can practice calling in imagery of the liquid blue blessing field—or any other imagery you feel would be helpful. If the session is incomplete, let the spirit know that you will return to help. Ask them to be patient, rest, and wait.

## Facilitating Spirit Release for a Client Attached to His Therapist

Delphine had an elderly male client who had been very attached to her. They had been doing deep early-childhood repair work when he became ill and then passed away.

In our consultation meeting two months after his death, Delphine reported that she was thinking about him all the time and grieving him. She was embarrassed about how much this was still affecting her life, and she sought to normalize her feelings. I sensed that something was amiss. I recalled how attached he was to her and how responsible she felt for his care. I wondered if he had not fully crossed over and was hanging around her, wanting something from her.

When I asked Delphine about this, she thought that it might be true—maybe he was still nearby and had not fully transitioned. I asked if she would like to explore this. She told me that she did.

I directed her to close her eyes and go inside. Then I asked her if she sensed that her client was still there with her. Delphine immediately answered yes, that he was there. I then asked her where she sensed him: Was he in front of her? To the right or left side, or behind her? She told me she sensed him to the right of her in front. I asked her to ask him if he knew he no longer had a body, that his body had died. She responded that he didn't know completely. When I inquired if she wanted to tell him that, she said yes and then communicated this silently in her mind.

At this point, after discerning that her client had indeed not transitioned and was with her, I wanted to find out what was keeping him from doing so. I asked her if there was something keeping him from crossing over.

Delphine immediately responded that yes, there was. He wanted her to go with him. He still wanted her to help him.

I asked her if she could let him know that she had a body and that it was not her time to leave. Could she tell him that they had completed their work together and that there were others who could help him in the next part of his journey? I then inquired if she could ask him to invite in any resources that could help him. They could be helping spirits, ancestors, or other resources that could help him with his transition. Delphine said yes. She then closed her eyes for several minutes. I could see emotions passing through her face, and her eyes were full of tears. There was obviously a lot happening during that time of silence.

When I checked in with her about what she experienced, she said that she saw white light—positive energy—coming for him, lifting him up. His father-figure cousin who passed away and his dog came and were holding him. These were resources he had tapped in during their EMDR therapy. His resource figures told him, "It's okay. You can't cling to her. We need to go to the next dimension." She said that she had positive light energy around her. She then declared out loud, "Thank you, and we need to separate."

At that moment I thought it was time to help him with the transition and asked if she could ask for a portal to open to the other dimension. She said to him, "We need to separate on some level." Seconds later she reported that he began to leave through the portal with the light resources. She was silent for a few minutes, processing internally the information that was coming to her. When I asked her what she noticed, she reported that he was not fully leaving. He was telling her that she had abandoned him. In response she told him that she didn't. "I did the best that I could while you were alive," she said. She told me that she was referring him to those who could help him with this part of his journey. She couldn't go with him. It was an appropriate referral. She was handing him over with love. After this she reported that he left through the portal. She felt relief.

Because I was concerned about her tendency to merge and lose herself with this client, I wanted to see how she was and if all of her energy was with her—that it had not transitioned with her client. I asked her if she felt all her energy with her. She responded that some of it had gone with him. Hearing this, I thought it was important for her to do an energy callback. I asked her if she could call back her energy to herself. Could she call all her energy in? I reinforced that by telling her that she had completed all her work with him.

She closed her eyes and imagined calling back her energy to herself for a few moments. Then a smile formed on her face. She told me that that felt good.

Because I sensed that she needed to fill with her own energy, as she had partially left herself and her client's energy had taken up some of the space in her, I asked her if she could imagine filling herself with her own energy, her True Self energy. Delphine nodded her head affirmatively. I asked her to invite her True Self energy to fill all the spaces in her body so that she was inhabiting herself. After a few moments she said that she could feel that and that it felt good. She said she felt much more grounded and filled with herself. I cautioned her to be gentle with herself and that she might be tired.

She should pay attention to how she felt and check in to see if her client had returned or had continued his journey. This had been sacred work we had done and to hold it as such.

Three months after this session, Delphine gave me permission to share her story and wrote the following:

> I feel so amazingly different and more clear-headed; it's like the feeling of one of those fairy tales where the curse has been reversed! From my feet up to my head, I feel the earth's grounding solidity, security, stability, and wildness. I can any-time I need to check my energy bubble and send that client's energy back to the parting in the sky, where he went with the helpers to his Peaceful Place, a blue throne room he'd created as a resource to be in with his dog. There is a felt sense energy boundary and separateness. He's in the other dimension, and I don't need to know all the details or imagine them; he's "good" and on his journey to the afterlife. My energy is my own again!!! I am still living life on life's terms with daily activities and challenges, of course, not walking on cloud nine, but I feel free of this merged situation that was going on for like six months plus! I no longer have to spend long periods feeling I'm fused with his thoughts, and memories of talking to him in long sessions. I am not responsible for holding him anymore, only with love and hope for his afterlife. I keep practicing the grounding cord exercise with other clients, and myself, and this helps conceptualize and strengthen the sovereign energy resource. I also know that I have the power, and I am in control. "I have Agency" to call in my energy and release the negative toxins or things that I don't want or need in my sphere and send them to be alchemized or composted, as you mention, into the earth for recycling. Also, sometimes I imagine a forcefield around my energy bubble, so if anything

unwanted tries to get in, the forcefield automatically just blasts it off into the universe.

## Facilitating Soul Release at Esalen Institute

Before I dive into telling of an experience with spirit release at Esalen, I want to share this preface from Shelley Pompana Spear Chief. Shelley is a psychotherapist who uses EMDR, somatic experiencing, traditional psychotherapy, hypnotherapy, and holistic therapy to help clients with an array of afflictions. As a First Nations Dakota woman married into the Blackfoot Nation who understands the challenges faced by First Nations people, Shelley also has an extensive background working with First Nations individuals with complex historical and ongoing traumatic experiences. She shares:

> Indigenous First Nations/Native American people historically used rituals to help people with healing. This often involved moving into another dimension realm with the use of healing rituals; drumming, singing, dancing, and herbal medicines. This isn't unique to Indigenous peoples of Turtle Island (known as Mother Earth) but practiced throughout many cultures with the rituals of drumming, rattles, singing, dancing, and herbal medicines. Ritual helps an individual move into an altered state, and it's not uncommon for spirits to present themselves that may need ancestral healing, bring messages, and look for guidance and support to cross over. Dr. Laurel Parnell speaks to this work and the importance of multidimensional ways of working and healing eloquently with genuine respect and tremendous healing and openness to honor all Indigenous people and their ancestors. One of the most important lessons shared with me by an Indigenous elder over thirty years ago when I was moving into my spiritual practices [is that] "spirit doesn't

have colour or judgement[;] it's pure energy—looking for help that comes in all kinds of forms." These weren't my words but the words of an elder who was mentoring me in spirit work.

## The Esalen Retreat

In the spring of 2023, I taught a weekend retreat at Esalen Institute in Big Sur, California, on Multidimensional Integrative Healing and EMDR. This was the first time I had taught these practices, and the purpose of the retreat was to learn about multidimensional ways of healing, especially when healing trauma using EMDR. All the women at this retreat were advanced practitioners and had spiritual practices. Several of the women in the group had been working and studying with spirit worker Jean Schneider to learn about energetic boundaries, spirit-release work, ancestral healing, and other practices that we have learned to integrate into our work with traumatized clients.

In addition, I had experienced and was learning to live after the terrible personal trauma and loss of my son. His death led me to this spirit work and working multidimensionally. Because his death was a homicide, I lost control over what the medical examiner for the city of San Francisco did with his remains. The medical examiner's responsibility was to investigate and determine the cause and manner of death and report to the city and county of San Francisco. Even after they had determined who killed my son, and the case was closed, they still held on to him. The lack of respect and consideration for my son and our family was shocking. At one point, when I was pleading with the medical examiner to release his remains, she asked me if I would like her to send me some of him!

I also do not believe that his remains were treated with respect. I did not know where they were, how they were being handled, or even if he was in one place. I was not able to collect his remains and do ritual, ceremony, and burial until eight months after his death. From this experience I learned the importance of ritual for both the dead and the living, as well as the powerlessness one feels when those rituals are denied.

I have felt a connection to the Indigenous people of the Americas whose people were killed and their children taken and disappeared, and who were denied their burial rituals. As a white woman of European heritage, I recognize the privilege I have, yet the experience of what was denied me after my son's death helped me empathize on a personal level with people who have historically been denied respect and basic human rights.

Prior to the retreat, I had been reading about the history of Native Americans in the United States, Canada, and California. This has been an interest and focus of study of mine for many years. I had also recently spent time in the Ecuadorian Amazon at the Sacred Headwaters with two Indigenous tribes and working with shamans there to help heal the sadness that would not lift. There I found the healing I needed, which along with the other things I was doing—including EMDR and the work with the spirit worker—has enabled me to teach and help others. All these things have deepened my connection to spirituality and openness to multiple dimensions for healing and understanding. This is to give some context for what might have attracted the spirit who came to us for help and how we found a way to help him from who we were and what we had been learning. I believe it is important to stress that we did not purposely invoke what happened. We came to learn and grow and to create community and connection. What happened in our group came to us, I believe, for a reason. I believe that the being/spirit wanted and needed help and recognized that we might be able to help him. We were also a circle of wise women who loved and honored one another. Many of us had had long, deep friendships over many years. We were all dedicated to healing trauma and working in multiple dimensions.

Our workshop began on a Friday evening at Esalen Institute during which nineteen women gathered in a beautiful room with large windows that opened to a view of the vast Pacific Ocean and sat in a circle. I began our workshop by reading an invocation out loud, which included honoring the Esselen people of the land on which we were working. The invocation is as follows:

I give thanks to those that I am about to invite.
I ask that the sacredness of our spaces opens up and shines, and for our spaces to come together as one space for the duration of our work today.
I invite your True Self and my True Self.
I invite the Divine to be present.
I invite Great Spirit, Mother Father God to be present.
I invite Great Mystery to be present.
I invite the Compassionate and Ascended Ancestors to be present and to support our work today if you are able to.
I invite the Ascended Great Teachers and Masters to be present, especially those that we have connections to and affiliations with.
I invite the Angels, the great beings of light, especially the archangels, the guardian angels, and the angels of healing.
I invite the Power Animals and Body Protectors, and I give thanks to them for loaning their power, their qualities, and for relationship.
I invite the Healing Spirits of all the realms and give thanks for the learning that I know is going to happen.
I invite the Elements: Earth, Water, Fire, Air, and Sacred Space . . . and I ask for a balancing of the Elements.
I give thanks to the Great Spirits of the Land and the spirits of our places, and I ask to be in harmony with you and to prosper here.

I give gratitude to the Ancestral Peoples of our lands, the Esselen people from these sacred lands, and ask for your blessing in this work.

I honor and respect all of the energies/beings/fields that are with us and our spaces that are not related to our work today, are unable to support our work today, or are not the right fit for our work today, and I ask for you to give us the gift of the space we need to do this work and to exit our spaces in a good way.

I ask for a sphere of protection and clarity and truth and light around us and around our workshop this weekend.

I give thanks in advance for the blessings that I know will happen here.

After the invocation, each person introduced herself and spoke about what she would like from the time together. We decided to begin with a structure but to allow space to adapt it as we went along, according to the needs of the group.

Later Friday evening, while in bed, one member of the group, Haleh, was visited by a spirit or entity, though at that time she did not realize what it was. Haleh has for some time been visited by spirits or entities who need or want help being released. Not only is she visited but she is often inhabited by them. She has been learning how to help these spirits cross over and ways of not being an open portal to being inhabited. Friday night she did not realize that this had occurred.

Saturday, I guided the various practices. We went through the grounding cord, energy bubble, and resourcing work. I then built on those practices with the True Self exercise.

I guided the women to imagine a grounding cord to connect them to earth energy and to draw the earth energy up into the channel in their backs, to create an energy bubble around them, to compassionately disinvite anything that did not belong to them, and to invite their resource figures to support them. After that, I led them in a visualization to connect with and fill with their True Self. After, Elizabeth, one of the group members, shared her experience. She had a lovely, very meaningful experience with the guided work, but then she reported seeing crossbars with yellow light behind them. She sensed a male entity/spirit that needed to be released and wanted to be freed. She had a strong sense to communicate this message to the group. She asked if any of the members were feeling blocked or trapped. Haleh reported that she was the one who felt blocked, and she could see the eyes of a man. She reported being visited by a male spirit who was trapped.

Julie, another group member, reported that she could sense what was happening with Haleh and identified the yellow light and blocked and sad emotions coming from Haleh behind her. Haleh identified the spirit as a man and described him to the group. I recognized the physical features of the male spirit that she was describing, including the way his hair was cut, as it resembled the haircuts Christian missionaries forced upon the Native peoples. Haleh began communicating to the male spirit, becoming a medium for his voice, answering questions asked by me and other women in the circle.

When I asked him if he knew he was dead, through Haleh he said no and began to cry. We offered our deepest sympathies, feeling with him the shock of what he just learned. He wanted to find where he came from and who he was. I continued to ask questions to help guide and understand who the male spirt was and what he needed. He wanted to know where he was from. When I asked him if he was from this land (Esalen), he said no, but from somewhere nearby that looked like here. I then got a picture in my mind's eye and asked if he was from the Carmel Mission. Haleh, Elizabeth, and others got an immediate yes, almost like an electric shock. This was helpful in guiding our questions for him.

We then knew that he was a Native man from the Carmel Mission who had died. Haleh kept getting the number eighty and did not know what that meant. Elizabeth and Julie stayed connected into Haleh's vision of the man's spirit and supported what he needed. Julie spoke of the eyes in the vision and asked Haleh to let him know that the women in the circle saw him and his people with eyes of love and respect for all Native people. Haleh continued to give voice to the male spirit and learned that he was a leader of a great number of Native people; he had a deep connection to the land and would not cross over until all of his people were able to cross over. He reported that the land was taken and his people desecrated, that they were lost and separated from their families and tribe.

We tried to help him cross over, but he seemed blocked. He said he needed ceremony, ritual for the dead that had been denied his people at the mission. Haleh stated that the male spirit requested we have a ceremony that would help the spirit transition. A song and dance came to Julie, which she spontaneously performed to help with the spirit transition. After this was done, the spirit left Haleh's body and she reported that he was next to her but still could not cross over.

When we asked him what was keeping him here, he mentioned he was looking for his wife and child. He was concerned about them. I kept seeing in my mind's eye wooden coffins with Christian crosses at the head of the graves. Haleh reported seeing enormous wooden crosses that were preventing the spirit and the others from crossing over. She also reported that he said he didn't want to go "up"—his people went down to the earth. Then an image of a condor came to me, and I recognized it as a psychopomp being—a being who helps spirits cross over. This resonated with the spirit, but the cross was still an obstacle to release. Suddenly, Haleh and several of us "saw" the cross transformed into a giant condor who carried the man's family, his people, and finally the man's spirit to the other side, where they were joyfully greeted by the spirits of their ancestors. Haleh, Julie, and Elizabeth reported witnessing hundreds of souls transitioning prior to the spirit making his final passage.

All the women in the circle stood in witness, held sacred space, and shared in the vision of the condor with outstretched wings as the spirits transitioned. Before their leader crossed over, he gave thanks to the circle for freeing him and his people to cross over. We stood in silence, honoring those who had come before them on this land. I led us in giving thanks for what transpired that day and the great need for the Native peoples' souls and land to be cleared, freed, and healed.

At the end of the retreat, I visited the Carmel Mission, which was about a half hour's drive from Esalen and is part of the history of the genocide perpetrated by the Spanish missionaries on the Native peoples of California. When I saw the cemetery, it looked much like what I had seen in my vision. There were two enormous wooden crosses there—one inside the cemetery and one outside. At the foot of each grave was a Christian cross. The mission was surrounded by a high wall that made it resemble a prison—there were even bars on the windows. When I sent Haleh the photos, she said the crosses were what she had seen too.

We all felt that we had participated in a sacred rite of passage. It was a profound honor.

# Concluding Thoughts

You have now been introduced to many ideas and practices that can serve to expand your awareness and help manage and release that which isn't yours. You have learned about how my spiritual and healing journey that included Buddhist and nondual teachers and teachings, as well as nature-based and spiritual practices from my spirit worker mentor, contributed to the development of Multidimensional Integrative Healing. Every one of my teachers emphasized that we are already the Buddha and wisdom resides in each of us. All have been loving and deeply compassionate—essential qualities in any teacher.

You learned about EMDR, Attachment-Focused EMDR, and Resource Tapping to clear traumas and integrate resources that can be of support to you in your life. Multidimensional Integrative Healing also includes a lens that embraces a broader cultural frame. As we become aware of the limitations of the one through which we view the world, we can open to the possibility of other ways of seeing our world and reality.

You have been introduced to Resource Tapping and several kinds of resources to support your life. They can be used whenever you need ease, comfort, courage, power, or wisdom. These resources include the Four Foundational Resources—Peaceful Place, Nurturing Figures, Protector Figures, and Wise Figures—and many others. You can call in spiritual resources and resources from nature for support. You can derive healing from resources that you discover in your ancestral lineages. Remember, all you need to do is call them up, feel the quality they represent for you, and then add bilateral stimulation. Our spiritual resources can be integrated into our daily meditation practice, which helps to reinforce the connection to them and enables us to contact them easily during challenging life situations. Nature resources can help to bring comfort, grounding, and support, connecting us to that which sustains us especially during turbulent, chaotic life events and emotional upset.

You have learned about energetic sovereignty—why we need to develop it and practical ways to do so. You were introduced to creating an energy bubble, grounding cord, and energetic containment room, as well as ways to assess if there are energies that don't belong to you in your bubble so that they can be compassionately released. All of these techniques can be used as part of a regular practice to help maintain your boundaries and keep you feeling clear in your own field of energy.

You were introduced to the concept of energetic cords—energetic pathways that hold contracts, agreements, and history—and ways to work with them so that you can take control over the information that is passing through them to you. By assessing if you have cord attachments from living people or even ancestors and lineages, you can take control over that information so that you don't allow what is unhealthy to pass from them to you or to future generations.

You learned ways to explore blocks to True Self—your essence, a core of goodness that has been there since the moment of conception or before—as well as methods for working with them in a variety of ways. By establishing a regular practice of connecting with your True Self, you can develop your inner knowing and alignment with your sense of what is right for you. You can learn to trust and listen to this inner compass to help guide you in your life.

You learned ways to develop work with dreams and EMDR, as well as with after-death communications. Finally, you learned how to recognize spirt attachments, why some of us are more likely to attract them, and ways to facilitate their release.

You can begin to use many of the practices you have learned as part of a daily meditation. Sitting quietly in the morning, you can call back your energy, use your grounding cord, ask for your energy bubble to surround you, and release anything that you discover there that isn't yours. You can call in your resources, anything you would like to provide support for your day, and tap them in. You can bring your awareness inward and connect with your True Self energy and ask for it to expand into all of you. You can notice anything that might block this expansion and inquire as to what it might be. You can call in resources to help remove blocks or notice if there is something from the past that is causing these blocks. You can set your intention for your day and perhaps sit silently for some time just being or doing any practices that you feel called to do that are helpful to you. If you find that there is something that feels like a spirit or soul attachment, you can inquire about what it might be and what it needs. Using the simple techniques outlined in this book, you can attempt to release it. If you need more help, there are spirit workers or others that you can contact who can be called on for this purpose.

The information that I have shared with you in these pages weaves threads of spiritual and energetic practices that serve to heal and support your inner knowing and help you find your way home to your True Self. Yet still there are times when you will need help from others to facilitate the healing or release you need. What I have offered here in these pages is limited by what I know. Please seek help from those who are wise, kind, compassionate, and skilled; who can help you release what isn't yours so that you can live from your True Self.

It is my greatest wish that what you learn here can bring greater love and healing to the vast, multidimensional web of connection that we are all part of. As we heal, it extends out in this web and healing energy radiates in all directions, including into the past and future. Recognizing this multidimensional interconnectedness is essential to healing ourselves, our world, and all the beings who inhabit it. May you and all beings be filled with Big Love expanding your heart with blissful energy radiating outward like a brilliant sun, dissolving perceived separateness between all living things. May we all live with this Big Love that is our true home.

# Acknowledgments

First of all, I wish to give my heartfelt thanks to my teachers and mentors who have inspired me with their wise and compassionate presence and teaching: Lama Thubten Yeshe, my root guru, whose transmission of Big Love continues to live through me and into the teaching and healing work I do. Jean Klein, beloved teacher whose words of wisdom resonated in the deep silence of his presence, reminding me of that which always is. Jack Kornfield, teacher and dear mentor, whose support through the difficult transition after the loss of the path was essential to finding my way forward. Suzanne Segal—psychologist, spiritual mentor, and girlfriend in the vastness—my heart will be forever grateful for your gift of normalization of living from our True Nature. Jean Schneider—mentor, healer, friend—I will be forever grateful for the healing you brought to my son, to me, and to my community of AF-EMDR therapist friends. You are the embodiment of a gifted spirit worker and bodhisattva, living without an ego, connected to the multidimensional universe, and working for the benefit of all beings.

Gracias a Manari Ushigua Santi—healer, shaman, protector of the rainforest—for the healing you gave me. With your great compassion and spiritual skill, you lifted the clouds of grief, returning me to life that included joy.

I give thanks to Francine Shapiro for the gift of EMDR that

continues to bring healing to our world. Thank you to my faculty and friends at the Parnell Institute and to my wonderful business manager, Angela Ruggiero, who holds it together and keeps things running.

I give great thanks to my beloved MDIH friends and spiritual sisters with whom we have shared our lives, our cases, and learned from one another: Haleh Rambod with a wise, compassionate heart, I deeply appreciate your love, friendship, laughter, and support through these years of great pain and challenge. Julie Probus-Schad—loving, talented teacher, with warm hugs and deep wisdom: You inspire me with how deep you can go with MDIH. Lizbeth Hamlin, multitalented woman of wisdom and great depth. Elena Felder—empathetic, openhearted, wise, and compassionate—you have been such a support to me, too, through this journey of healing and learning. Vinutha Mohan, thank you for your love, deep spiritual wisdom, guidance, and support. I will be forever grateful to you for helping me find Jean Schneider, a gift beyond measure. To Karin Weidenmueller, wise woman and member of our MDIH group, whose contributions always provide expanded ways of understanding. To Elizabeth Cruickshank for your contributions to this book and the courage to step into your spiritual wisdom.

I give thanks to Shelley Pompana Spear Chief—First Nations Dakota Woman, EMDR therapist, and Indigenous elder—for your friendship, sharing of our complicated multidimensional lives, and contribution to this book.

I give thanks to my husband, Pierre Antoine Blais, for your love and support through the great ups and downs of our long marriage, and to my granddaughter, Katya Laurel Kudrya, whose loving heart and wisdom beyond her years is inspiring and deeply gratifying to witness. To my son Etienne Perez-Parnell, whose love and support through the first year following the loss of his brother will always be remembered with deep appreciation.

I give thanks to my wise ancestors, helping spirits, and any other spiritual helpers from other dimensions who have supported the actualization of this book.

I give thanks to the Coastal Miwok People and the land where I live—the creek, trees, sacred mountain, and all of the animals who live here.

I have gratitude for the clients and colleagues who contributed their stories of healing, including Evelyn Lee, Navroop Sood, and others.

My gratitude to the wonderful supportive team at Sounds True. To Jaime Schwalb, thank you for believing in this book and helping to shepherd it through the first stages to acceptance. Angela Wix, my editor: I appreciate how masterful you are at both editing and providing constructive feedback to make *Releasing What Isn't Yours* a better book. My appreciation to the group that created the beautiful cover and to the team of Angela Wix, Tami Simon, and Jaime Schwalb, who helped find the title to fit the book I was writing.

Finally, I send my heartfelt gratitude to my son Catono Raymond Perez, whose support in spirit form has inspired and guided this work. I miss you every day and love you with all my heart.

# Multidimensional Integrative Healing Practices

## Part Two: Accessing the Resources of Multidimensional Integrative Healing

### Chapter 5: Your Four Foundational Resources

Tapping In Resources 55
Tapping In a Peaceful Place 59
Tapping In Your Nurturing Figures 61
Tapping In Your Protector Figures 63
Tapping In Your Wise Figures 65
Tapping In Inner-Wisdom Figures 66
Tapping In Your Resource Team 68

### Chapter 6: Spiritual and Natural Resources

Tapping In a Higher Power 75
Tapping In Spiritual Figures 76
Tapping In Spiritual Experiences 79
Tapping In Spiritual Teachings 81
Tapping In Nature 84
Tapping In Big Love 88

### Chapter 7: Ancestral Resources

Finding Healthy, Whole Ancestral Time 95
Bridging to Ancestral Resilience 99
Finding a Wise Ancestor/Guide 100
Resourcing from the Ancestral Land 103
Journeying to the Ancestral Well or Spring 106

## Part Three: Developing Energetic Sovereignty

### Chapter 8: Basic Tools for Energetic Sovereignty

Grounding Cord Guided Imagery Script 113
Locating and Assessing the Energy Bubble 116
Clearing Unwanted or Unwholesome Energies from the Energy Bubble 120
Steps for Creating an Energetic Containment Room 127

### Chapter 9: Working with Energetic Cords

Steps for Working with Energetic Cords 133
Working with Ancestral Cords or Energetic Patterns 138

### Chapter 10 Working with the True Self

Tapping In the True Self 146
Exploring Blocks to Living Fully 152
Working with the True Self 154

### Chapter 11: Bringing Together Multidimensional Integrative Healing Practices

Uniting the Practices of MDIH 163

## Part Four: Dimensions of Spirit Work

### Chapter 12: The Importance of Dreamwork in Multidimensional Integrative Healing

Exploring the Most Compelling Part of a Dream 174
Processing a Dream with Many Parts 175

### Chapter 13: EMDR and After-Death Communication

Some Recommendations for Receiving After-Death Communication 186

### Chapter 14: Recognizing and Assessing Spirit Attachments

Assessing the Signs and Using Inquiry to Determine What Has Attached 195
Assessing for Spirit Attachments Using Clear and Open Space Method 197

# Notes

## Introduction to Multidimensional Integrative Healing

1. Roger Cohen, "Who's a 'Colonizer'? How an Old Word Became a New Weapon," *The New York Times*, December 10, 2023, nytimes.com/2023/12/10/world/europe/colonialist-word-gaza-ukraine.html.

## Chapter 1: Spiritual Influences and Teachers

1. Suzanne Segal, *Collision with the Infinite: A Life Beyond the Personal Self* (New Sarum Press, 2020).

## Chapter 5: Your Four Foundational Resources

1. Shelley Spear Chief and Moses Spear Chief, *Eagle Wings Flapping: Beaver Learns to Manage Big Emotions* (Tellwell Talent, 2022).

## Chapter 7: Ancestral Resources

1. Daniel Foor, *Ancestral Medicine: Rituals for Personal and Family Healing* (Bear & Company, 2017).

# About the Author

Laurel Parnell, PhD, is the executive director of the Parnell Institute and the developer of Attachment-Focused EMDR, Resource Tapping, and Multidimensional Integrative Healing. As a psychologist, teacher, and author with over forty years' experience as a meditator and spiritual practitioner, Laurel has been actively integrating psychological and spiritual work throughout her career. She served on the faculty of the California Institute for Integral Studies and John F. Kennedy University in the Graduate School for the Study of Human Consciousness, and she has been presenting and teaching nationally and internationally for thirty years. An innovator and expert in EMDR (Eye Movement Desensitization and Reprocessing), she has trained thousands of clinicians in the United States and abroad. She is the author of six other books: *Rewiring the Addicted Brain with EMDR-Based Treatment*, *Attachment-Focused EMDR: Healing Relational Trauma*, *Tapping In*, *A Therapist's Guide to EMDR*, *EMDR in the Treatment of Adults Abused as Children*, and *Transforming Trauma: EMDR*.

Laurel is passionate about helping people, traveling to countries around the world to teach and consult about healing trauma while also learning from them about their cultures and how she might meet their needs. She brings a transpersonal/spiritual perspective to her work, which she calls Multidimensional Integrative Healing.

She has presented on this topic at conferences, workshops, and retreats. She lives in Northern California with her husband, granddaughter, and rambunctious tabby cat.

# About Sounds True Books

Sounds True was founded in 1985 by Tami Simon with a clear mandate: to disseminate spiritual wisdom. Since starting out as a project with one woman and her tape recorder, Sounds True has grown into a mission-driven learning and media company, partnering with many of the leading wisdom teachers and visionaries of our time.

Every Sounds True Book is designed to not only provide information to a reader but to also to embody the quality of a wisdom transmission, unlocking our greatest capacities to love, serve, and uplift others.

Sounds True Books are part of St. Martin's Essentials, an imprint of Macmillan Publishers.